CARTOON
CAKES

CARTOON
CAKES

WORLDWIDE PUBLISHING

TM

DEBBIE BROWN

MEREHURST

Contents

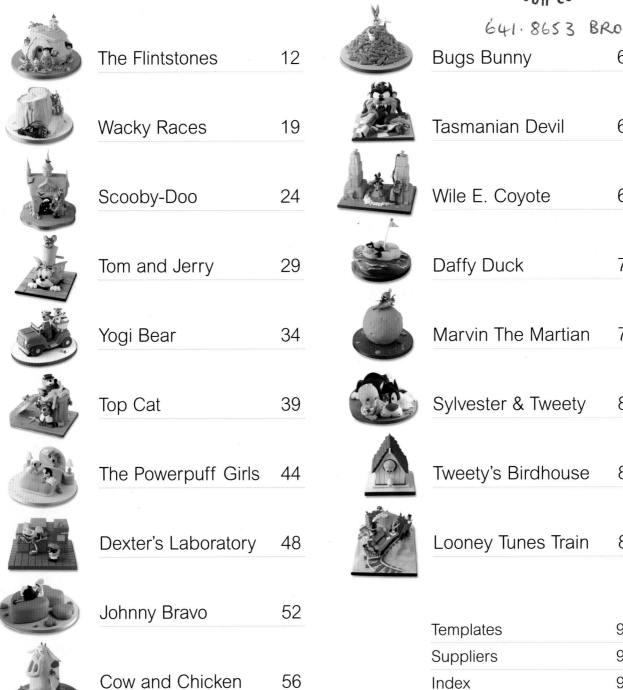

Dedication

Introduction

For years I have wanted to write a cake decorating book about the ever popular Warner Bros., Hanna-Barbera and Cartoon Network characters and so I am very glad that I have finally had the opportunity to do so. Although the characters are quite detailed, each project has been carefully thought out so that it is possible for beginners and experienced cake decorators alike to get great results. The easy-to-follow instructions tell how to trim away from a baked cake to reveal a shape that will become either the actual character or an appropriate scene to put the modelled characters in. The modelling is simplified too, with basic shapes building up to reveal a character right before your eyes.

Most projects in this book can be altered if time is short. Bear in mind that a simplified cake can look just as good as one that is highly detailed. For example, by placing only Fred on The Flintstones cake (see pp.12–18) you will give him more emphasis. Then by adding Dino into one of the front windows licking his cheek you will add some fun and humour. Use this book as inspiration for your own designs and you won't be disappointed with the results.

Remember, a special cake makes an important celebration complete, whether as a centrepiece on the party table, or presented by the waiter at a restaurant. To see the recipient's joy at being given such a special gift is worth all the time and effort that was put into making it.

Recipes and Materials

Madeira can be cut and shaped easily.

Add flavourings such as chocolate.

Sugarpaste is used as the cake covering.

MADEIRA SPONGE CAKE

The secret of successful cake decorating is to use a firm, moist cake that can be cut and shaped without crumbling. Madeira cake is a good choice and can be flavoured for variety. To make a madeira cake, see p.11 then follow the steps below.

1 Preheat the oven to 160–170°C/ 325°F/Gas 3, then grease and line the bakeware.

2 Sift the self-raising and the plain/ all-purpose flour together in a bowl. Then put the soft margarine and caster/superfine sugar in a large bowl and beat until the mixture is fluffy.

3 Add the eggs to the mixture, one at a time with a spoonful of the flour, beating well after each addition. Then add flavourings if required.

4 Using a large spoon, fold the remaining flour into the mixture. Spoon the mixture into the bakeware, then make a dip in the top of the mixture with the back of the spoon.

5 Bake in the centre of the oven until a skewer inserted in the middle comes out clean.

6 Leave the cake to stand for about five minutes, then turn out onto a wire rack and leave to cool. When cold, store in an airtight container.

SUGARPASTE

I recommend using ready-made sugarpaste (rolled fondant), which is of high quality and is available from cake-decorating suppliers (see p.95) and supermarkets. You can, if you wish to, also make your own.

To make 625g (1¼lb)
- 1 egg white made up from dried egg albumen
- 30ml (2tbsp) liquid glucose
- 625g (1¼lb/4½ cups) icing (confectioner's) sugar
- A little white vegetable fat (shortening) if required

1 Put the egg white and liquid glucose into a bowl, using a warm spoon for the liquid glucose.

2 Sift the icing (confectioner's) sugar into the bowl, adding a little at a time and stirring continuously until the mixture thickens.

MADEIRA CAKE FLAVOURINGS

- **Vanilla** Simply add 5ml (1tsp) of vanilla essence/extract to every 6-egg mixture.
- **Lemon** Add the grated rind or the juice of 1 lemon to a 6-egg mixture.
- **Almond** Add 5ml (1tsp) of almond essence and 30–45ml (2–3tbsp) of ground almonds to every 6-egg mixture.
- **Chocolate** Add 30–45ml (2–3tbsp) of unsweetened cocoa powder mixed in 15ml (1tbsp) of milk to a 6-egg mixture.
- **Chocolate swirl cake** Fold 155g (5oz) of dark melted cooking chocolate into each 6-egg madeira mixture, until a swirling effect is achieved. For a marbled effect, gently stir in the chocolate. Spoon the mixture into the required bakeware and follow baking instructions.

3 Turn out the paste onto a worksurface dusted with icing sugar and knead until it is smooth and pliable. If the paste is dry and cracked, fold in a little vegetable fat (shortening) and knead again.

4 Put it into a polythene bag, or double wrap the paste in cling film (plastic wrap), and store in an airtight container until you are ready to use it.

BUTTERCREAM

As well as making a delicious filling between layers of cake, a thin coat of buttercream spread all over the cake fills any small gaps and also provides a smooth surface on which to apply the sugarpaste. Buttercream can also be flavoured.

To make about 500g (1lb/2 cups)
• 125g (4oz/½ cup) butter, softened or soft margarine
• 15ml (1tbsp) milk
• 375g (12oz/2¾ cups) icing (confectioner's) sugar

1 Put the butter or soft margarine into a mixing bowl. Add the milk and/or any flavouring required (see box, below).

2 Sift the icing (confectioner's) sugar into a bowl, a little at a time, and beat well after each addition, until all the sugar has been incorporated into it and the buttercream has a light, creamy texture.

3 Store the buttercream in an airtight container until required.

MODELLING PASTE

Modelling paste is made by incorporating an edible gum into sugarpaste. The gum is available in powder form and is easily kneaded into the sugarpaste, which makes the paste much firmer but still pliable. You can model items using just sugarpaste, but modelling paste keeps its shape well and dries much harder, giving strength to your finished work.

The natural gum, gum tragacanth, or the manmade alternative, CMC (carboxy methyl cellulose), were employed to make the modelling paste that is used in this book. Both are widely used in the food industry as thickeners. Gum tragacanth needs a little time after it has been kneaded into sugarpaste before the gum starts to work, usually around 4–8 hours. CMC, on the other hand, starts to work virtually straight away and is slightly stronger and cheaper. There are also some ready-made modelling pastes available that give good results. All these items are available from cake-decorating suppliers.

To make 500g (1lb) of modelling paste
• 10ml (2tsp) gum tragacanth or 5–7ml (1–1½tsp) CMC
• 500g (1lb) sugarpaste (rolled fondant)

1 Put the gum on a worksurface and knead it into the sugarpaste.

2 Double wrap the paste in cling film (plastic wrap) or polythene and keep airtight.

Buttercream provides a smooth surface, ready for the sugarpaste coating.

Modelling paste keeps its shape well.

Modelling paste is used to make the various characters.

BUTTERCREAM FLAVOURINGS
• Vanilla Add 5ml (1tsp) vanilla essence (extract).
• Lemon Replace the milk with 15ml (1tbsp) fresh lemon juice.
• Chocolate Mix the milk and 30ml (2tbsp) unsweetened cocoa powder to a paste and add to the mixture.
• Coffee Mix the milk and 15ml (1tbsp) instant coffee powder to a paste and add to the buttercream mixture.

Royal icing is used for piping details.

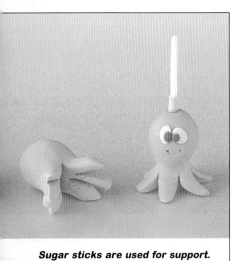

Sugar sticks are used for support.

Sugar glue is applied with a paintbrush.

ROYAL ICING

Royal icing is used to pipe details with and also to stick items firmly in place. Ready-made royal icing can be obtained in powder form (follow the instructions on the packet). You may prefer to make your own in the following way.

To make about 75g (2½oz)
• 5ml (1 level tsp) egg albumen
• 15ml (3tsp) water
• 65–70g (about 2½oz) icing (confectioner's) sugar

1 Put the egg albumen into a bowl. Add the water and stir until dissolved. Beat in the icing (confectioner's) sugar a little at a time until the icing is firm and glossy and forms peaks if the spoon is pulled out.

2 Place a damp cloth over the top of the bowl until you are ready to use it – this will stop the icing from crusting.

SUGAR STICKS

Support is sometimes required when building up modelled items. Sugar sticks can be used to help hold such pieces in place and are quick and easy to make, although some drying time is required. Alternatively, raw, dried spaghetti can be used.

To make around 10–20 sugar sticks
• 5ml (1 level tsp) royal icing
• 1.25ml (¼tsp) CMC or gum tragacanth

Knead the gum into the royal icing until the mixture thickens and forms a paste. Roll it out and cut it into different-sized strips of various lengths using a clean straight-bladed knife. To stop untidy edges and crumbling occurring, roll the knife down through the paste. Alternatively, you can just roll the paste into thin sausage shapes. Leave the sticks to dry for around 4–8 hours before use.

SUGAR GLUE

Sugar glue is required to stick pieces of sugarpaste (rolled fondant) together. Egg white made up from powdered egg albumen is a good glue, as is royal icing or sugarpaste and water mixed together.

Alternatively, a glue made from gum arabic is popular, which is available from cake-decorating suppliers. Mix 5ml (1tsp) gum arabic powder with a few drops of water to make a paste and keep airtight in the refrigerator.

To stick sugarpaste pieces together, slightly dampen the paste with sugar glue using a fine paintbrush. Gently press them into position, holding for a few moments. Small pieces of foam sponge can be used to support them while they are drying.

FOOD COLOURING

Food colouring can be obtained from cake-decorating suppliers and many supermarkets. When deep or brightly coloured sugarpaste is required, I recommend using paste food colourings as they are more concentrated. Food colouring in liquid form is also available, but only use these for pastel shades as they will make the paste sticky. Food colouring in powder form is good for dusting your cake to achieve subtle shades.

STORING THE DECORATED CAKE

Store in a cardboard cake box in a warm, dry room. NEVER leave in the refrigerator as the dampness will make the cake spoil.

Basic Techniques

CUTTING & SHAPING CAKES

To sculpt cake into different shapes, use a sharp, serrated knife. Cut a little at a time, shaving off small pieces until you have the required shape. If you shave off more than you need, pieces of cake can be stuck back on with a little buttercream but take care not to do this too much because it may cause the sugarpaste (rolled fondant) to slip when applied.

BALANCE

When building up a high cake, make sure that each layer is completely straight and that the cake is balanced. If part of the cake is left only slightly uneven it will look much worse when covered with sugarpaste and may cause the cake to lean.

COLOURING SUGARPASTE

Add food colouring to the sugarpaste a little at a time with a cocktail stick (toothpick). Knead it into the sugarpaste, adding more until you have the required shade. Wear plastic gloves as the colouring can temporarily stain hands. Alternatively, pre-coloured sugarpaste packs are now readily obtainable from cake-decorating suppliers and supermarkets.

PREPARING SUGARPASTE

Knead the paste thoroughly until it is warm and pliable before rolling it out onto a worksurface covered with a sprinkling of icing (confectioner's) sugar. Keep moving the paste around so that it does not stick and roll it to a thickness of 3–4mm (⅛in), unless otherwise stated.

To lift a large piece of rolled-out sugarpaste, lay a large rolling pin on the centre and flip the paste over it. Lift it, position, then roll the paste into

place. Use a sharp, plain-edged knife to cut the paste. To avoid the paste 'pulling', cut cleanly downwards. Keep wiping the blade to remove excess, or a layer of paste will build up and make cuts untidy. When the sugarpaste is dry, polish the surface with your hands to remove excess icing sugar and to give it a sheen.

COVERING THE BOARD

Roll out the sugarpaste, then lift it over the board to cover. Use a cake smoother to give a smooth surface. If the paste has not stuck to the board, lift the sugarpaste around the edge and moisten with a damp paintbrush. Trim any excess downwards with a sharp knife. You may wish to remove the sugarpaste from the area of the board on which the cake will sit. Because the cake is moist, the sugarpaste beneath has a tendency to become sticky. Leave boards to dry for at least 12 hours.

COVERING THE CAKE

Spread a layer of buttercream over the surface of the cake to help the sugarpaste stick. Roll out sugarpaste and cover the cake where required, smoothing around the shape and trimming any excess. Rub the surface with a cake smoother to produce a smooth surface.

MODELLING CARTOON HANDS & ARMS

Cartoon hands only have three fingers and a thumb because the animation looks much better this way. For this reason, cartoon hands are a little easier to model than full hands are.

A cartoon hand is made by first rolling the modelling paste into a ball, then into a teardrop shape. The

Shave off the crust before shaping the cake.

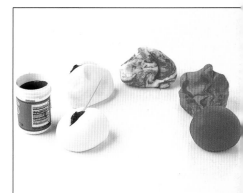

Use a cocktail stick when adding colour.

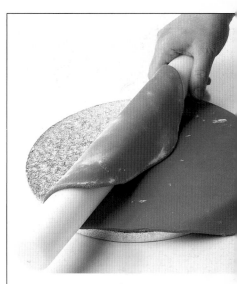

Cover the board using sugarpaste.

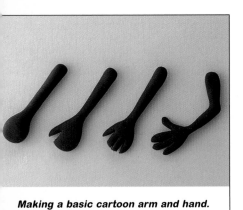

Making a basic cartoon arm and hand.

Paint fine details such as eyelashes using diluted food colouring.

A selection of tins and ovenproof bowls used to bake the cakes.

teardrop is then flattened gently, and during this process you should take care not to indent it. Cut a thumb first, slightly to one side, and pull down away from the hand. Make two cuts at the top to separate into three fingers. Gently twist each finger to lengthen it a little and press down on the tip of each to round them off. Cartoon hands are often narrow at the base and very full at the fingertip, so use a cocktail stick (toothpick) between each finger at the base. Press down on the tip of each finger to round off.

The fingers are then bent into position. Bear in mind that a natural-looking hand bends a little, so press gently into the palm. The fingers should be close together with the thumb positioned a little away from them and tucked slightly underneath. Holding the hand at the wrist area will help to round off the hand.

Sometimes an arm is also required. Start by rolling the modelling paste into a sausage shape. Pinch a wrist gently at one end, rounding off a hand. Press down gently on this rounded end to flatten it, and then follow the instructions given above. By doing this, you will complete the hand and arm, although occasionally an elbow must also be modelled. In these cases, gently pinch in halfway between the wrist and shoulder and pinch out at the back to bend the arm.

PAINTING DETAIL ON PASTE

Liquid food colouring can be used for painting directly onto the paste, but as most projects throughout this book require paste colours, you can dilute a little of this easily with a drop of water.

To make it easier to paint fine details correctly, make sure that you use a good-quality paintbrush, preferably one made of sable. Most brushes have numbers gauging their sizes; a fine brush is usually between 00 and 1 and a medium paintbrush 2–3. When painting onto models, the brush should only be damp with colour, so blot any excess with a dry cloth or some absorbent kitchen paper before applying it to your figure.

Ideally the paste should be completely dry before you paint onto its surface. This is because it is much easier to remove painted mistakes from the surface of paste that has had time to dry. If you do make a mistake, wipe it away with a damp cloth or use a clean damp paintbrush to lift away the colour a little at a time.

SPECIALIST EQUIPMENT

Ball/Bone Tool These are basic modelling tools with rounded ends used to indent paste when making holes, eye sockets and ears. The ball tool has a large and small ball at each end and the bone tool has a slightly curved large and small ball, which also indents a teardrop.

Cake Smoother This is used to create a smooth surface on sugarpaste. The type with a handle is the most useful. Smooth it over the surface of the paste in a circular motion to level it.

Cutters Paste cutters come in many different shapes and sizes. Circle and square cutters are the most useful.

Foam A foam sheet is useful for placing modelled items on. It also helps the underside to dry as air can circulate underneath. Small pieces of foam sponge are used to support items until dry.

Cake Quantities Chart

Refer to p.6 for madeira cake instructions.

Cake	Page	Bakeware	Eggs	Self-raising flour	Plain/all-purpose flour	Butter/soft margarine	Caster/superfine sugar	Baking time
Wacky Races	19	Two 15cm (6in) round tins and 10cm (4in) round tin. Evenly fill each tin	5	315g (10oz/ 2½ cups)	155g (5oz/ 1¼ cups)	315g (10oz/ 1¼ cups)	315g (10oz/ 1¼ cups)	50 min– 1 hour
Yogi Bear Powerpuff Girls Dexter's Lab Cow & Chicken Wile E. Coyote	34 44 48 56 68	20cm (8in) square tin	5	315g (10oz/ 2½ cups)	155g (5oz/ 1¼ cups)	315g (10oz/ 1¼ cups)	315g (10oz/ 1¼ cups)	1¼–1½ hours
Bugs Bunny	60	20cm (8in) round tin	5	315g (10oz/ 2½ cups)	155g (5oz/ 1¼ cups)	315g (10oz/ 1¼ cups)	315g (10oz/ 1¼ cups)	1¼–1½ hours
Marvin The Martian	76	Two 1l (2 pint) ovenproof bowls. Divide the mixture equally between them	5	315g (10oz/ 2½ cups)	155g (5oz/ 1¼ cups)	315g (10oz/ 1¼ cups)	315g (10oz/ 1¼ cups)	1¼–1½ hours
Tweety's Birdhouse	84	25cm (10in) square tin	5	315g (10oz/ 2½ cups)	155g (5oz/ 1¼ cups)	315g (10oz/ 1¼ cups)	315g (10oz/ 1¼ cups)	50 min– 1 hour
Daffy Duck	72	25cm (10in) round tin	5	315g (10oz/ 2½ cups)	155g (5oz/ 1¼ cups)	315g (10oz/ 1¼ cups)	315g (10oz/ 1¼ cups)	50 min– 1 hour
Johnny Bravo	52	Two 15cm (6in) heart-shaped tins. Divide the mixture equally between them	6	375g (12oz/ 3 cups)	185g (6oz/ 1½ cups)	375g (12oz/ 1½ cups)	375g (12oz/ 1½ cups)	1¼–1½ hours
Top Cat	39	Two 15cm (6in) round tins. Divide the mixture equally between them	6	375g (12oz/ 3 cups)	185g (6oz/ 1½ cups)	375g (12oz/ 1½ cups)	375g (12oz/ 1½ cups)	1¼–1½ hours
Sylvester and Tweety	80	15cm (6in) square tin, 1l (2 pint) ovenproof bowl and 220ml (7fl oz/1 cup) ovenproof bowl. Put half the mixture into the square tin and the remaining mixture into the two bowls	6	375g (12oz/ 3 cups)	185g (6oz/ 1½ cups)	375g (12oz/ 1½ cups)	375g (12oz/ 1½ cups)	For tin and large bowl: 1¼ hours For small bowl: ½ hour
Tom and Jerry	29	1.5l (3 pint) ovenproof bowl and 18cm (7in) round tin. Put two-thirds of the mixture into the bowl and the rest of it into the tin	6	375g (12oz/ 3 cups)	185g (6oz/ 1½ cups)	375g (12oz/ 1½ cups)	375g (12oz/ 1½ cups)	For bowl: 1½ hours For tin: 1 hour
The Flintstones	12	Two 20cm (8in) round tins. Divide the mixture equally between them	6	375g (12oz/ 3 cups)	185g (6oz/ 1½ cups)	375g (12oz/ 1½ cups)	375g (12oz/ 1½ cups)	1 hour
Scooby-Doo Tasmanian Devil Looney Tunes Train	24 64 87	25cm (10in) square tin	6	375g (12oz/ 3 cups)	185g (6oz/ 1½ cups)	375g (12oz/ 1½ cups)	375g (12oz/ 1½ cups)	1 hour

THE FLINTSTONES ™

Millions of fans around the world love this stone-age animation. To make sure that everyone's favourite is here, I have included all the characters from the Flintstone and Rubble families.

CAKE AND DECORATION

2 x 20cm (8in) round cakes (see p.11)

30cm (12in) round cake board

1.67kg (3lb 5½oz) sugarpaste (rolled fondant)

Green, golden brown, turquoise, black, chestnut brown, yellow, red and pink food colouring pastes

410g (13oz/1½ cups) buttercream

Icing (confectioner's) sugar in a sugar shaker

Sugar glue

360g (11¾oz) modelling paste

Two sugar sticks or lengths of raw, dried spaghetti

EQUIPMENT

Large rolling pin

Sharp knife

Cake smoother

Templates (see p.93)

Small, pointed scissors

Small brush for glue

Ruler

No.4 plain piping tube (tip)

Small pieces of foam sponge

Fine paintbrush

Dinner knife

A few cocktail sticks (toothpicks)

Miniature circle cutter

PREPARING THE CAKE AND BOARD

1 Colour 375g (12oz) of the sugarpaste (rolled fondant) green. Roll this out and cover the cake board, trimming the excess from the edge, and put it aside to dry. Trim the crust from each cake then slice the top flat on one cake and trim a rounded top on the other, following where the cake has risen down to the base. Place the cakes one on top of the other.

2 Trim around the base of the cake, cutting in at an inward angle to round it off. Cut the roof to slope slightly downwards on one side and at the front to make a flat area for the doorway. Sandwich all layers together with buttercream then spread a layer over the surface.

CREATING THE HOUSE

3 Colour 1.25kg (2½lb) of the sugarpaste cream using a little golden brown food colouring paste. Add a bit more and knead until a mottled effect is obtained. Roll out 640g (1lb 4½oz) of the paste and cover the cake, smoothing around the shape and trimming the excess. To create the rock effect, smooth angular ridges around the cake using the side of a cake smoother. Place the cake on the board, slightly towards the back. Cut out the door and windows at the front using the templates (see p.93), removing the sugarpaste.

4 Roll out 125g (4oz) of the cream paste and make the surface uneven. Cut out the larger part of the door surround (see p.93) and stick

Shape the cakes and place one on top of the other.

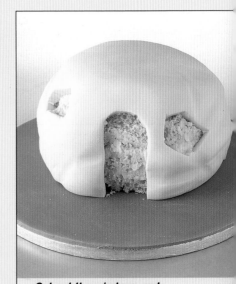

Cut out the windows and door using the templates.

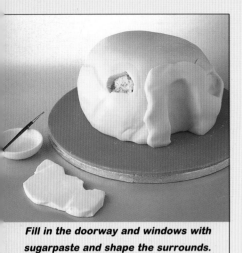

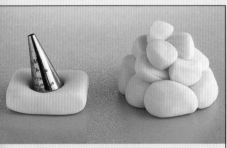

Fill in the doorway and windows with sugarpaste and shape the surrounds.

Stack rocks to create the chimney and cut out the top with a piping tube.

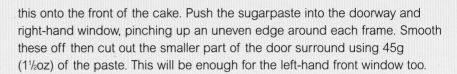

this onto the front of the cake. Push the sugarpaste into the doorway and right-hand window, pinching up an uneven edge around each frame. Smooth these off then cut out the smaller part of the door surround using 45g (1½oz) of the paste. This will be enough for the left-hand front window too.

5 Colour 30g (1oz) of the modelling paste turquoise. Thinly roll out 22g (¾oz) and cut a door using the template (see p.93). Mark lines on it with a ruler, cut out the round window with the end of a no.4 piping tube and then stick the door into the doorway. Model a doorknob with turquoise trimmings. Colour 30g (1oz) of the modelling paste black. Using the window templates (see p.93) and half of the paste, thinly roll out and cut window shapes to fill each window, and cut out a circle to fill the door window.

6 Colour 45g (1½oz) of the sugarpaste golden brown. Thinly roll out and cut the pathway using the template (see p.93) and stick this in position. With golden brown trimmings, model tiny pebbles and stick these on the pathway.

7 The roof is made in two parts (see p.93). The base is a thick wedge made up of 280g (9oz) of cream sugarpaste. This is rolled out thickly and made to look layered by marking uneven lines around the edge with the back of a knife. You should also mark angular ridges on the top and then secure it in place as before with sugar glue. For the top part, roll out another 45g (1½oz) of the paste and cut out the shape using the template. Stick this in position.

8 With 22g (¾oz) of the cream sugarpaste, model different-sized rocks to edge the pathway. Using 30g (1oz), model more rocks and stick these into a circle for the base of the chimney, then build it up, narrowing it at the top. Model another 7g (¼oz) into an oblong for the chimney top and cut out a circle from the centre using the end of the piping tube (tip).

9 For the doorsteps, roll out and cut a thick 2.5 x 4cm (1 x 1½in) oblong for the bottom step using 15g (½oz) of the cream sugarpaste. Pinch this gently around the edge to soften it and make it slightly uneven. Make a smaller top step using 7g (¼oz) of the paste and stick this in place. Make the planters with the remaining cream, pushing into the top of each to hollow out slightly.

10 Colour 45g (1½oz) of the modelling paste chestnut brown. For the tree, roll the paste into a sausage that tapers at one end. Using scissors, snip cuts around it that graduate in size then stick it in place. Colour 22g (¾oz) of the modelling paste green. Using three quarters, roll teardrop shapes for the tree and shorter ones to fill the plant pots. Use pieces of foam sponge to support the leaves. Colour 45g (1½oz) of the modelling paste orange using yellow food colouring paste with a touch of red. Using 15g (½oz), thinly roll out and cut curtains using the template (see p.93). Roll the paintbrush handle over the surface of each to create pleats and stick in place.

MODELLING FRED

11 Fred is modelled flat and is then positioned on the cake when he is dry. First colour 125g (4oz) of the modelling paste flesh-coloured using golden brown food colouring paste with a touch of pink. Also colour 7g (¼oz) a slightly

14

deeper flesh colour. For his body, roll 30g (1oz) of the pale flesh-coloured paste into a teardrop shape and cut a 'v' from the point to shape his neck.

12 Split 7g (¼oz) of the pale flesh-coloured paste in half. To make a leg, roll one half into a thick sausage and bend it in half. Pinch gently at the bend to shape a heel and indent around the ankle to narrow and round off the top of the leg. Press down on the toe area and cut twice to separate the toes. Pinch each toe gently to round off and press the end of a paintbrush into the big toe to mark the nail. Make the opposite leg in exactly the same way. Then stick the two legs together, making sure that the feet turn out, and stick them into position on the body.

13 Thinly roll out 15g (½oz) of the orange modelling paste and cut out Fred's costume using the template (see p.93). Wrap this around his body to cover it completely, tucking the excess around the back. For his head, model a rounded teardrop shape using 15g (½oz) of the pale flesh-coloured modelling paste. Cut off the rounded point of the teardrop to make a flat area for his hair. Rub the edge to round it off, then stick it onto his body. Smooth the chin area down to fit the 'v'-shaped neckline.

14 Using a pea-sized amount of the turquoise modelling paste, thinly roll out and cut his neck tie using the template (see p.93). Stick this in place with a small knot joining the pieces. Use 7g (¼oz) of the flesh-coloured modelling paste split in half to make his arms. Roll into sausage shapes and pinch gently to round off one end of each. See pp.9–10 for how to make hands, but keep the fingers shorter. Stick in place with the palms turning backwards.

15 For Fred's stubble, model a flattened diamond shape using just over half of the darker flesh-coloured modelling paste and stick this onto his face. Press the flat part of a dinner knife centrally into the surface to mark his smile and then indent dimples onto the stubble area with the tip of the piping tube pressed in at an angle.

16 Stick on two flattened circles of white for eyes, each with a black pupil. Model a teardrop-shaped nose and two tiny ball-shaped ears, pinching each ear to a point. Model black teardrops for his hair that graduate in size. When his hair is in place, model a tiny sausage of black and stick this onto his parting. Push into the centre to indent and make both ends stick up. Model four triangular shapes for his costume.

MAKING DINO

17 Colour 7g (¼oz) of the modelling paste deep pink. Using a tiny amount, model Dino's oval-shaped eyes and hollow them in the centre with the end of a paintbrush. Fill each with white eyes and black pupils and set them aside. With the rest of the deep

Here are all the pieces that are needed to make Fred.

When you make Fred's neck tie, fit it together with a small knot in the middle.

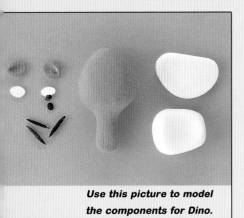

Use this picture to model the components for Dino.

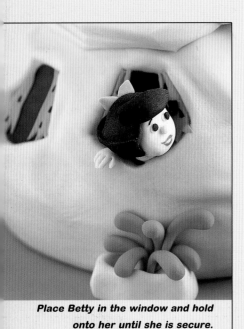

Place Betty in the window and hold onto her until she is secure.

The sides of Wilma's hair are made from spirals of orange paste.

pink, model his head and neck using the photograph as a guide. Push the tip of a cocktail stick (toothpick) into the top of his head to make holes for his black hair to fit into later on.

18 For his muzzle, colour just under 7g (¼oz) of the modelling paste very pale pink. Split this into two pieces so that one is slightly larger than the other. Roll the smaller piece into a tapering sausage and press it flat. Stick this onto Dino's head to make his mouth area. With the second piece, shape his muzzle and stick this high onto the mouth area, smoothing in either side to remove the join. Using a cocktail stick, dimple the corners of the mouth and indent nostrils into the front. Stick the eyes on and put Dino aside to dry.

BETTY

19 Use just over 7g (¼oz) of the pale flesh-coloured modelling paste to model Betty. First model her tiny neck, and then roll the remainder into a ball for her head and indent the eye area by rolling gently with the paintbrush handle. With 7g (¼oz) of the black paste, put a pea-sized amount aside and then roll out the remainder into a strip for her hair. Stick this in place wrapped around the back of her head and turn it up at the bottom, stroking it up and outwards at the sides. Shape the front piece of her hair with the left-over piece and stick this in place. Model tiny flattened white and black circles to make eyes and roll a ball nose. Stick her in place and hold for a few moments until secure.

20 With a pea-sized amount of pale flesh-coloured paste, model a teardrop shape. Press it flat and cut a thumb to one side. Cut twice into the top to separate fingers and pinch each to a point before sticking on the window ledge. Colour a small piece of modelling paste pale blue and model two tiny triangular shapes for her bow.

MAKING WILMA

21 For Wilma's head, model an oblong shape using just over 7g (¼oz) of the pale flesh-coloured modelling paste. Pinch this gently all the way round at one end to shape her small neck. The opposite end needs to be high at the back to build up her hair, so gently pinch it up. Then press down on her face to flatten it slightly. Use 7g (¼oz) of the orange modelling paste for her hair. Model a flattened oval of orange to cover the back of her head and a flattened circle for the top. Position them and moisten the point where the two pieces meet with sugar glue. Smooth it over to remove the join.

22 Roll a thin sausage using a pea-sized amount of orange and spiral it around, pinching two angular ends. Stick this onto the side of her head, smoothing it in as before. Make two more for the other side and front. Roll

another thin sausage and spiral it upward into a bun to create the top. Stick the head in place and then hold for a few moments until it is secure.

23 Model white balls of modelling paste and stick these in a circle around her neck. Make one hand with a pea-sized amount of the pale flesh-coloured paste as for Betty's. Model a ball-shaped nose and two oval-shaped eyes.

Here are the components for Barney. He is made in a similar way to Fred.

BARNEY

24 Model Barney's head in the same way as Fred's, using 15g (½oz) of the pale flesh-coloured modelling paste. Make the stubble in the same way, but cut a straight line across the top of it. For his mouth, stick on a flattened circle of deep flesh-coloured paste and then smooth into the top to remove the join, leaving a semicircle for his smile. Indent in each corner using the piping tube pressed in at an angle. Make his nose and ears as Fred's.

25 Stick Barney's head at a window, holding him for a few moments until secure. Then colour 7g (¼oz) of the modelling paste dark golden brown. Using the template (see p.93) cut out Barney's costume and wrap it around the bottom of his head, tucking the ends around the back. Reserve the trimmings for later. Colour 7g (¼oz) of the modelling paste pale yellow and make his hair. With pea-sized amounts of pale flesh-coloured paste, make two hands following the components picture as a guide (see top, right) and stick these on the window ledge.

Follow this step-by-step guide to make Pebbles, ensuring her feet are turned outwards slightly.

MAKING PEBBLES

26 For Pebbles' head, roll just under 7g (¼oz) of the pale flesh-coloured modelling paste into a ball and indent the eye area by rolling gently with the paintbrush handle. Push in a cocktail stick underneath to make a hole for the sugar stick or length of raw, dried spaghetti to slot into later.

27 With one quarter of the remaining turquoise modelling paste, make Pebbles' knickers. Roll a small sausage and pinch at either end, pushing your thumb each side to hollow it out slightly. Stroke a small curve into the top and stick in a pea-sized oval of pale flesh for her tummy, indenting her belly button with the tip of a cocktail stick. To make her legs, use pea-sized amounts of the pale flesh-coloured paste. Roll a small sausage, rounding off one end. Bend and pinch out a heel. Press either side of the foot to lengthen and mark toes with a knife. Make the opposite leg and stick them both into her knickers with each foot turned outwards.

28 For her top, shape the remaining green modelling paste into a teardrop and hollow out the full end by pinching an edge. Press down onto the point with the paintbrush handle to create the neck area. Stick this onto her body.

29 For her arms, split a pea-sized amount of pale flesh-coloured in half and model as before, keeping the arms short and childlike. Stick a minute piece of pale paste to fill her neck area. Push a sugar stick down through her body leaving 1.5cm (½in) protruding. Push her head on and secure with glue.

Push Pebbles' top up slightly at the front to reveal her tummy.

30 Her hair is built up using long flattened teardrops of orange modelling paste. Build it up from the back leaving spaces for ears. Press a flattened ball on top for her topknot with two small teardrops twisted together. For the bone pieces either side, shape small balls of white modelling paste and indent a line with a cocktail stick. For her face, stick two tiny flattened black circles for eyes, a ball nose and two tiny ears.

BAMM BAMM

31 Model Bamm Bamm's head as Pebbles' but indent a smile using the miniature circle cutter pressed in at an angle. Indent again just underneath his smile using the tip of the no.4 plain piping tube at an angle. Make his legs as Pebbles'. For his body, model a teardrop shape using just under 7g (¼oz) of the pale flesh-coloured modelling paste and then stick this in place against his legs. Press the point down to flatten the neck area.

32 Colour 7g (¼oz) of the modelling paste pale brown. Roll out and cut a strip for his costume, trimming a ragged edge. Reserve the trimmings for later. Wrap this around his body covering the top of his legs, securing it at the back with sugar glue. Gently rub the join until it is removed and press around the waist to remove the ridge.

Use this picture as a guide to modelling the post box.

33 Make two arms like Pebbles'. Model a tiny bone as before but make it out of one piece and stick it onto his front. Roll out the dark golden brown trimmings and cut a thin strip for the strap, making tiny cuts down each side. Stick this over his shoulder diagonally going down the front and back. Wrap the front end over the centre of the bone, and then trim the excess away.

34 Push a sugar stick down through his body as before and gently stick his head on. Build up the hair using white modelling paste. Model a tiny peaked cap with the pale brown trimmings by shaping a tiny dome for the cap and a tapering sausage pressed flat for the peak. Model two tiny flattened circles of white for his eyes and make pupils, nose and ears as before.

FINISHING TOUCHES

35 To make Bamm Bamm's club, colour the remaining modelling paste dark green using green with a touch of brown food colouring paste. Roll this into a long teardrop shape and texture the surface by scratching it gently with a cocktail stick. With the remaining orange and turquoise, make the post box. For the top, roll the turquoise into a sausage and hollow it out completely by pushing the end of the paintbrush handle through it. Roll it over the worksurface to neaten and then smooth it around the outside. Indent lines and wood grain using a knife. Model the orange paste to create the base, marking wood grain as before.

Stick Dino into the top of the chimney and then add his hair.

36 To finish the detailing, dilute a little black food colouring paste with a little water. Paint the costumes, curtains and facial details using the fine paintbrush. (If you prefer you can model some of these details, but painting is the easiest option.) Then stick Dino into the chimney. For his hair, roll tiny sausages that taper at each end and slot these into the holes on top of his head using sugar glue to secure. Dilute some red and paint Betty and Wilma's smiles. Stick Fred in place resting against the house, with Pebbles and Bamm Bamm on the path.

WACKY RACES

With so many different vehicles in the race it would be too time consuming to include all of them, so I have picked the two most popular, which appeal to boys and girls respectively.

CAKE AND DECORATION

2 x 15cm (6in) round cakes, 1 x 10cm (4in) round cake (see p.11)

25cm (10in) round cake board

1.25kg (2½lb) sugarpaste (rolled fondant)

Cream, golden brown, black, navy blue, mauve, red, green, yellow and pink food colouring pastes

440g (14oz/1¾ cups) buttercream

200g (6½oz) modelling paste

Icing (confectioner's) sugar in a sugar shaker

Sugar glue

EQUIPMENT

Large and small rolling pins

Sharp knife

Templates (see p.94)

Small brush for glue

A few cocktail sticks (toothpicks)

A piece of foam sponge

Ball or bone tool

Miniature circle cutter

2.5cm (1in) circle cutter

Fine paintbrush

TIME SAVING TIP

Decorate with just one Wacky Races vehicle or use toy vehicles instead to save even more time.

CUTTING AND COVERING THE CAKE

1 Colour 470g (15oz) of the sugarpaste (rolled fondant) cream. Roll out 315g (10oz) and use to cover the cake board, trimming the excess from around the base. Using your finger, indent lines around the outside edge to resemble wheel markings and put aside to dry.

2 Trim the crusts from each cake and slice the tops flat. Put the two larger cakes one on top of the other. Using the cutting diagram as a guide (see p.94), trim a wedge from the smaller cake to make a roadway from the top down to the base. Then position the cake on top of the other two cakes. Trim the roadway into the bottom two in the same way, so that the road spirals down and around the cake.

3 Sandwich the layers together with buttercream and spread a layer over the surface of the whole cake to help the sugarpaste stick. Position the cake centrally on the cake board.

4 Using 30g (1oz) of the cream sugarpaste, roll out and cover the top of the cake with a circle of cream sugarpaste. Roll out another 125g (4oz) and cut a strip to cover the roadway, smoothing the joins closed at each end. Using your finger, indent a spiral on the top of the cake and lines down the road.

5 Colour the remaining sugarpaste golden brown. Roll out around 75–155g (2½–5oz) at a time and use these pieces to cover the cake

Trim a wedge out of the smaller cake to create the top part of the roadway.

Sandwich each of the cakes together with buttercream.

19

Texture the paste using a paintbrush before applying to the sides of the cake.

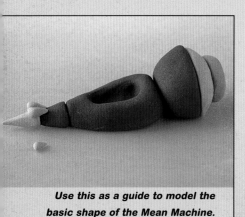

Use this as a guide to model the basic shape of the Mean Machine.

This step-by-step photograph shows you how to make each wheel and the shape of the back wheel arches.

sides, smoothing all the joins closed. Trim away any excess and press with your hands to create ridges, incorporating the joins to hide them. Pinch an uneven, rocky edge around the top edge, a little higher than the roadway. For the rock fall, cut away the sugarpaste to leave a minimal covering and mark an uneven surface with the end of a paintbrush. Cut cracks into it with a knife. Use golden brown trimmings to model small rocks and place randomly.

MODELLING THE MEAN MACHINE

6 Colour 22g (¾oz) of the modelling paste black and 7g (¼oz) dark golden brown. Using the template (see p.94) and 7g (¼oz) of the black paste, roll out and cut the car roof shape. Cut out the centre for the shape using thinly rolled out dark golden brown paste and stick it onto the black roof, indenting lines in it using a knife. Put the roof aside to dry.

7 Colour 60g (2oz) of the modelling paste navy blue. Using the photograph as a guide, model the central piece of the Mean Machine using half of the paste. Model a dome shape with another 22g (¾oz) of paste to make up the back piece and use half of the remainder to shape the front.

8 Colour 15g (½oz) of the modelling paste mauve. Using half of it, model a shallow dome shape for the back of the Mean Machine. Split the remaining mauve in half, shape a rounded dome and model a pointed teardrop for the front, edging it with smaller teardrops made from the remaining mauve. Indent detailing on the vehicle with the tip of a cocktail stick (toothpick). Use a piece of foam sponge as support until the pieces are dry.

9 Colour a small piece of the modelling paste dark grey and make four wheels, indenting in the centre of each with the small end of a ball or bone tool. Split 7g (¼oz) of the black paste in half and use one half to make the wheel arches. Shape the other half into a flattened circle to fill the seat area.

10 Model a small teardrop of black using a pea-sized amount and press it flat to make the point at the front of the car. Using dark golden brown, model another slightly smaller teardrop and press it flat before sticking it onto the black point. Cut the bottom of the shape straight and stick it upright onto the front of the car, bending it over at the top.

11 At the back of the car, stick a small flattened circle of black paste in the centre. On top of this stick a flattened circle of dark golden brown, followed by a slightly larger flattened circle indented in the centre using the large end of a ball or bone tool. Indent small holes around it using a cocktail stick. Then edge the whole of the back with small black teardrop shapes, pressing the point of each flat. Decorate the black teardrop shapes with golden brown circles as before, but make them much smaller and use the small end of the ball or bone tool to indent them.

12 For the pointed hubcaps, colour a pea-sized amount of the modelling paste pale grey and press flattened circles onto the centre of each wheel. Indent in the centre of each using the end of a paintbrush. Roll four tiny pointed teardrops and stick them in place pointing upwards.

13 Colour 60g (2oz) of the modelling paste red. For the rings on the sides of the car, model two tiny flattened circles and press in the centre of them with the bone tool to make indents. Then fill the indented parts with navy blue. Colour a tiny amount of the modelling paste green and use it for the oval-shaped sign on the side of the car. Make another sign and put it aside. Stick the car in position on the cake board, without the roof.

DICK DASTARDLY AND MUTTLEY

14 To make Dick Dastardly, colour just over a pea-sized amount of the modelling paste cream. Put aside a tiny ball. From the remainder, make his long nose and a teardrop shape for his head. Pinch up the point of the teardrop to make his chin, curving it up and round. Flatten the top.

15 Model the top of his hat with red modelling paste and stick the head onto the hat. Press a minute ball of white paste flat and cut it in half for his eyes. With the remaining navy blue, cut a collar and position it.

16 Colour just under 7g (¼oz) of the modelling paste pale blue. Model two tiny white glasses and stick a small lens onto the centre of each using pale blue paste. With a little red, model a flattened teardrop for his peak and cut off the point. Stick this in place at the base of his hat, resting on his nose. Position Dastardly in the car, leaving room for Muttley. For his moustache, roll a thin sausage of black and taper each end to a point. Use the damp glue brush to pick it up and stick it in place.

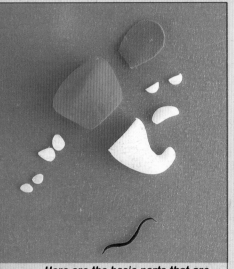

Here are the basic parts that are needed to make Dick Dastardly's head.

17 Colour just over a pea-sized amount of modelling paste dark yellow using a touch each of golden brown and yellow food colouring pastes. To make Muttley's head, shape a teardrop and bend the point up. Roll the back of a knife along the rounded end to mark his wide smile and also mark a vertical line on his muzzle. For hair, flatten a tiny circle and cut 'v' shapes from around the edge and stick this onto the top of his head. Cut into the flattened black teardrop shapes to make his ears and then model his black nose. Stick Muttley in place next to Dastardly and add a tiny modelled paw so that it hangs over the edge of the vehicle. Make his eyes and two tiny pointed teeth out of white paste.

MAKING THE COMPACT PUSSYCAT

18 Using just under 45g (1½oz) of the red modelling paste make the car chassis, indenting in the centre to make the seat area. Mark two lines either side for the doors. Split just under 7g (¼oz) of the red into three pieces. With one, model a pair of lips for the front of the car. With the other two, model wheel arches and cut the ends off at an angle.

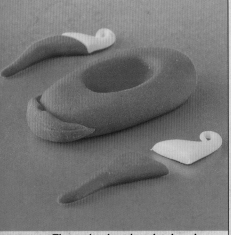

The main chassis, wheel arches and lips for the Compact Pussycat.

19 Colour just over 7g (¼oz) of the modelling paste yellow. Complete the wheel arches by curling some of the yellow around at the top and put them aside until set. Colour 7g (¼oz) of the modelling paste deep pink. Using half, roll four small wheels and stick them in place with a tiny yellow ball as a hubcap in the centre of each.

20 To make the large front yellow wheel arches, roll sausage shapes that taper at either end. Stick these into position so that they edge the two front wheels and curl them into a spiral at the front. Next, stick the back wheel arches in place. To decorate the bonnet, cut a tiny strip of yellow and cut out semicircles on either side of it using the miniature circle cutter.

21 Thinly roll out a little more yellow paste and cut a circle using the 2.5cm (1in) circle cutter. Press this into the seat area. Using a small amount of the pale blue paste, model a semicircle for the seat and indent radiating lines onto it with the back of a knife. Roll a tiny yellow sausage and bend it round to make the steering wheel. Stick the green sign on the side of the car that was made earlier.

22 Roll a 7g (¼oz) ball of white modelling paste and cut it in half to make the parasol. Thinly roll out a little red paste and cut strips to decorate the top of the parasol and also model a bow. Roll a sausage of deep pink paste, press this flat and indent it down either side to make a frill. Stick this around the bottom of the parasol, smoothing the join closed.

23 With a pea-sized amount of pink modelling paste, roll a group of tiny balls and press them as flat as possible using icing (confectioner's) sugar on your hands to prevent them from sticking. Cut each in half and stick the semicircles so that they edge the bottom of the wheel arches.

PENELOPE PITSTOP

24 Use the remaining pink to make Penelope's helmet and collar. For her helmet, model a rounded teardrop shape and also roll a tiny tapering sausage for the visor. For her collar, which is modelled so that it will sit into the seat, make a teardrop shape. Hollow it out and pinch up an edge at the fullest end. Using the remaining cream, stick a flattened oval onto the front of the helmet, slightly indenting the eye area and adding a nose.

25 Roll out and cut a tiny white strip to decorate her helmet and stick on two white pieces for glasses with blue lenses. Stick the visor in place, edging the top of her face with a tiny strip of yellow for her fringe. Stick Penelope's head into her collar and place her in the car seat. Model her long hair at the back by rolling a ball of yellow and then pinching either end into points, one longer than the other. Curl the longest end around at the bottom. Stick blue 'eyes' onto the two wheel arches at the front.

FINISHING TOUCHES

26 Cut the points from the cocktail stick and push it down into the Compact Pussycat. Carefully push on the parasol, securing it with sugar glue. When the cake is dry, dilute navy blue food colouring paste and paint stripes on Dastardly's hat. Dilute black food colouring paste and paint the facial details, the 'W' on the green signs, the '5' and the outline and eyelashes around Compact Pussycat's 'eyes'. Dilute a little red and paint Penelope's smile. Stick a minute ball of black trimmings onto both ends of the Mean Machine's roof. Moisten them with sugar glue and then stick the roof in place, using Dastardly's head as a support for it in the centre.

The components that are needed to build up Penelope Pitstop.

Paint the number five and other fine details onto the cars as finishing touches.

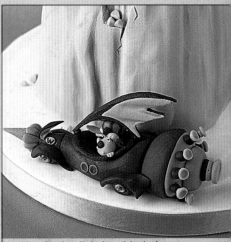

Use Dastardly's head to help support the Mean Machine's roof.

SCOOBY-DOO!

Scooby-Doo and Shaggy are always having ghostly encounters in their popular cartoon. Here it looks as though they are just about to have another spine chilling experience!

CAKE AND DECORATION

25cm (10in) square cake (see p.11)

25cm (10in) petal-shaped cake board

1.6kg (3lb 3½oz) sugarpaste (rolled fondant)

Black, blue, red, green, cream, golden brown, turquoise and yellow food colouring pastes

500g (1lb/2 cups) buttercream

Icing (confectioner's) sugar in a sugar shaker

Sugar glue

125g (4oz) modelling paste

45g (1½oz) royal icing

Edible sparkle powder (petal dust/blossom tint)

EQUIPMENT

Large rolling pin

Sharp knife

Template (see p.93)

Small piece of card

Scissors

Foam sheet

No.0 plain piping tube (tip)

Paper piping bag

Cocktail stick (toothpick)

Miniature circle cutter

Fine paintbrush

COVERING THE CAKE AND BOARD

1 Colour 315g (10oz) of the sugarpaste (rolled fondant) dark grey using black food colouring paste with a touch of blue. Roll this out and cover the cake board completely, trimming excess from around the edge. Gently press the rolling pin over the surface to create ripples, smooth the edge and put it aside to dry.

2 Trim the crust from the cake and slice the top flat. Cut the cake into four equal squares and put one on top of the other, making sure that each one is level. To shape the roof, trim a wedge from the front and back of the cake, cutting down and outwards to take off the top edge from the second layer.

3 Trim around the base of the cake so that the sides slope at an inwards angle. Sandwich the layers together with buttercream, then spread a thin layer over the surface of the cake.

4 Colour 1.25kg (2½lb) of the sugarpaste a slightly paler shade of grey. Roll out 125g (4oz) and place the back of the cake down onto it. Cut around, leaving the roof uncovered. The sugarpaste will stick to the surface when the cake is replaced onto its base.

5 Cover the sides of the cake in the same way, using 170g (5½oz) of the grey paste for each side. Sugar glue the join closed and then rub gently with your fingers to remove the join line. Position the cake on the cake board.

Trim the cake around the base so the sides slope inwards.

Thinly roll out black sugarpaste and use to cover the door area.

MAKING THE CASTLE

6 Colour the remaining sugarpaste black. Thinly roll out and cover the front of the cake at the doorway only. Roll out 125g (4oz) of the grey sugarpaste and cut a piece to cover the front of the cake, smoothing the joins closed as before. Using the template (see p.93), cut out the doorway and remove the sugarpaste, revealing the black underneath.

7 Roll out 45g (1½oz) of the grey and cut a strip to cover the top of the cake. Then roll out 125g (4oz) more and cut an oblong that is slightly larger than the roof. As the cake sides are fuller at the top, the roof shape should taper. Cover the opposite side of the roof in the same way. Cut a little dip at the bottom of the roof where Shaggy and Scooby-Doo's heads will rest.

8 To make the dormer, thickly roll out 75g (2½oz) of the grey and cut the shape using the template (see p.93). Put this upright and slice down the back at an inwards angle so that it sits flush on the roof. Roll out another 30g (1oz) of the grey and cut the dormer roof.

9 To mark cracks on the dormer, indent with the tip of the knife, and then cut lines. To make slits, cut a small piece of card into a 1.5cm (½in) square, fold it in half and push the folded side into the front of the dormer.

10 Using 220g (7oz) of the grey sugarpaste, model the turrets and turret roofs. Fold a 2.5cm (1in) square of card in half and use the fold to indent the large slit on the central turret. With the darker grey trimmings, shape different-sized flattened 'stones' and stick these randomly over the surface of the cake. With the remaining grey, model rocks and use these to decorate around the base of the cake.

11 Using 7g (¼oz) of white modelling paste, first model flattened circles, cutting them off at an angle to make the three sets of eyes at the doorway. Then roll the remainder into a sausage, rounding off one end. Press the rounded end flat and cut a thumb, slightly to one side, then cut fingers across the top. Pinch and bend the hand round into a fist and stick this against the doorway, holding it for a few moments until it is secure.

MAKING SHAGGY AND SCOOBY-DOO

12 Shaggy and Scooby-Doo are assembled flat, preferably on a foam sheet, and are only positioned when they are completely dry. Colour just under 7g (¼oz) of the modelling paste dark red using red food colouring paste with a touch of blue added to it. Split this in half and roll long teardrop shapes, pinching around the full end to hollow out and create Shaggy's bell-bottoms. Push in at the back and pinch at the front to shape his knees and then stick the knees together.

13 Colour 15g (½oz) of the modelling paste green and model Shaggy's top, cutting the sleeves at either side and hollowing out the space for his arms to slot into later. Smooth

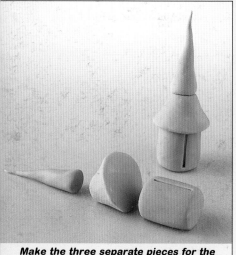

Make the three separate pieces for the turrets and then stick them together.

Model rocks and use them to decorate around the whole of the cake.

gently to remove ridges. Pinch around the base to hollow it out and fit it over the trousers, making sure you secure it with sugar glue. Push in at the top with the tip of the knife to create a 'v'-shaped neckline.

14 Colour just over 7g (¼oz) of the modelling paste cream. Model Shaggy's neck by rolling a tiny piece of cream into a sausage, pinching one end into a point and then sticking it into the top of the t-shirt.

15 Colour 60g (2oz) of the modelling paste dark golden brown. Using 22g (¾oz), shape Scooby-Doo's body and stick this onto the front of Shaggy so that the top is in line with Shaggy's neck area. (Leave some of his green t-shirt showing underneath.)

16 Split 7g (¼oz) of the dark golden brown paste in half. Put one piece aside to make the other front leg later. Roll the other piece into a sausage and round off one end to make his paw. Indent three times into the end using a knife. Push down at the shoulder area to enlarge it and press it flatter. Pinch gently to bend the arm halfway down for the elbow and stick it in place around Shaggy's shoulders, securing the paw onto his t-shirt.

17 With a small piece of cream modelling paste, shape Shaggy's head. Make a dip in the centre for his eye area and stick on a small nose and ears. To open his mouth, gently push in with the end of a paintbrush. Colour 15g (½oz) of the modelling paste black. Make two tiny flattened circles of white for eyes and then stick on two tiny black pupils and eyebrows.

18 For his hair, colour a little modelling paste pale golden brown and shape it into different-sized flattened teardrop shapes. Stick this on his head, building up the layers little by little. Stick the head in place resting on Scooby-Doo's arm for support. Make Scooby-Doo's opposite front leg as before and stick this in place, wrapping the paw around Shaggy's neck. Smooth the shoulder into the surface of his body using sugar glue, and then rub the surface with icing (confectioner's) sugar to remove the join.

19 For Shaggy's shoes, split just under 7g (¼oz) of the black paste in half and model two teardrop shapes. Cut a 'v' in one side of each to separate the heels and pinch gently to make them more angular. Stick these into each bell-bottom with the toes pointing towards each other.

20 Split just over 7g (¼oz) of the dark golden brown modelling paste in half. To make one of Scooby-Doo's back legs, roll one of the pieces into a sausage and round off one end. Press the rounded end flatter and pinch either side to lengthen and round off the toe area, and then mark it three times using a knife. Pinch out a heel at the back. Press down at the opposite end to enlarge the thigh. Bend the leg halfway up to make the knee and stick the leg in place, smoothing the join closed as before. Make the second back leg.

21 Put aside a tiny piece of cream modelling paste, and then split the remainder in half and use it to make Shaggy's arms. To make an arm, roll a sausage shape and round off one end, pressing it flatter. Cut a thumb and

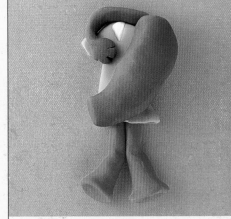
Build up the two figures together on a flat surface.

These are the components that are needed to make Shaggy's head and hair.

A close-up to help when building up the two figures.

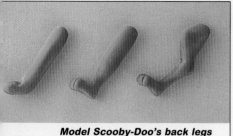

Model Scooby-Doo's back legs following this step-by-step guide.

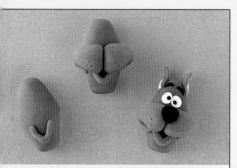

Build up Scooby-Doo's head by first modelling his mouth, muzzle and whiskers. Then add the details such as ears, eyes, nose and eyebrows.

Dust the cake with edible sparkle powder to make it shimmer.

fingers and twist each gently to lengthen them. Stick the arm in place holding onto Scooby-Doo's legs. Make another arm in the same way. Roll a sausage of dark golden brown paste for Scooby's tail and stick this in place, curling upwards.

22 For Scooby-Doo's collar, colour a small piece of modelling paste turquoise. Roll out and cut a tiny diamond for a name tag, then shape the remainder of the paste into a flattened circle for his collar and stick in position. Colour a little royal icing yellow. Using the piping tube (tip) and bag, pipe 'SD' onto the centre of the diamond and an outline. Also pipe a line on the front of the collar and then stick the name tag just below it.

23 Model Scooby-Doo's head using 7g (¼oz) of the golden brown modelling paste. For his mouth, model a sausage tapering at either end and stick this onto his face curling upwards. Indent in the centre to open his mouth. Model two teardrop shapes for his muzzle and stick these either side of his face, curving round each point to form the sides of his mouth. Indent whiskers with the tip of a cocktail stick (toothpick).

24 Model two pointed ears, indenting in the centre of each and filling them with a patch of cream. Squeeze at the base to fold them in a little, and then stick them in place. With white and black paste, make Scooby-Doo's eyebrows, eyes and pupils. Then stick his head in position supported by Shaggy's head. Press black modelling paste over his back for patches and then model his triangular-shaped nose.

FINISHING TOUCHES

25 Use the remaining black and white modelling paste to make bats. For wings, model flattened teardrop shapes. Cut one side of each so that it is angular and on the underside cut out semicircles using the miniature circle cutter. Shape tiny flattened circles for the heads. Make their eyes with the pupils close together to create a 'cartoon' look.

26 When the cake is dry, dilute a little black food colouring paste with water. Using the fine paintbrush, paint Shaggy's bristles on his chin. Colour the remaining royal icing dark grey. Spread this over the back of Shaggy then press him into position at the front of the cake, holding him for a few moments until he is secure. As a finishing touch, dust the cake with the sparkle powder (petal dust/blossom tint).

TOM and JERRY ™

The pranks that Tom and Jerry play on each other are great, harmless fun. I've incorporated the slapstick humour that has made them the most popular cartoon duo ever.

CAKE AND DECORATION

1.5l (3 pint) bowl-shaped cake and 18cm (7in) round cake (see p.11)

30cm (12in) square cake board

470g (15oz) modelling paste

Black, brown, orange, yellow, green, pink and red food colouring pastes

Icing (confectioner's) sugar in a sugar shaker

Sugar glue

1.7kg (3½lb) sugarpaste (rolled fondant)

440g (14oz/1¾ cups) buttercream

EQUIPMENT

Large rolling pin

Sharp knife

Small glue brush

30cm (12in) ruler

Templates (see p.94)

Cocktail sticks (toothpicks)

Firm bristle paintbrush

8cm (3in) circle cutter

Ball or bone tool

A few pieces of foam sponge

20–25cm (8–10in) food safe dowelling

Star cutter

DECORATING THE CAKE BOARD

1 Colour 100g (3½oz) of the modelling paste black. Put aside 22g (¾oz) then thinly roll out the remainder and cover the centre of the cake board only, using sugar glue to secure. To prevent the covering sticking, dust the black area with icing (confectioner's) sugar. Roll out 500g (1lb) of the white sugarpaste (rolled fondant) and cover the cake board completely, trimming the excess from around the edges. Using a ruler, mark three even lines across the board to indent floorboards and also mark vertical lines for the board joins. Use the template (see p.94) to cut out the centre and remove the white sugarpaste, revealing the black that is beneath it.

Peel away the white sugarpaste to reveal the black underneath.

2 Mark lines across the cake board for wood grain and create a ragged edge in the centre. Then mark nails at the joins using a cocktail stick (toothpick). Dilute brown and orange food colouring pastes together with water until the mixture becomes translucent. Using the firm paintbrush, paint a thin coat of this colour over the floorboards in the direction of the wood grain. The colour will initially seep into the marked lines to highlight the wood grain effect and resist the top surface. Leave this to dry for 10 minutes before painting over it again and then put the board aside to dry.

29

Cut three circles from the round cake and use to form the mallet.

Tom's muzzle is formed from two large teardrop shapes.

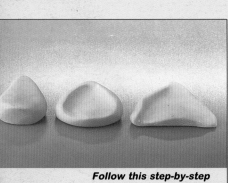

Follow this step-by-step sequence to create the shape of Tom's ears.

3 The bowl-shaped cake is used to make Tom's head. Where the cake has risen, trim away the crust slightly, leaving a flat area for the base of Tom's head, but still keep a rounded edge. Slice two layers into the cake and sandwich back together with buttercream.

4 Trim the crust from the round cake and slice the top flat. Cut out three circles using the circle cutter and stack them on top of each other. Trim all the way around, narrowing at one end to make the mallet shape. Fill each of the layers with buttercream and then spread a thin layer of buttercream over both cakes to help the sugarpaste stick.

MODELLING TOM

5 Colour 875g (1¾lb) of the sugarpaste grey using a little black food colouring paste. Roll out 750g (1½lb) and use it to cover the bowl-shaped cake completely, smoothing down and around the shape and trimming away any excess. If the cake board is dry, position the cake on the centre of the cake board. (If not, go on to the next steps, putting the features in place first before positioning the cake on the board.)

6 Colour just under 15g (½oz) of the sugarpaste pale grey. Use the template (see p.94), to roll out and cut the fur shape between Tom's eyes. Stick it into position on the centre of his face, smoothing the edge to remove the ridge.

7 Colour 15g (½oz) of the sugarpaste pale yellow and 7g (¼oz) green. Split the yellow and green in half and model Tom's eyes using the template (see p.94) as a guide. Make Tom's pupils using a pea-sized amount of the black modelling paste for each.

8 Use half of the white sugarpaste that was removed from the cake board and shape it into an oval. Stick this onto the bottom of Tom's face to create his mouth area. Make an opening for his mouth by pushing the large end of a ball or bone tool into the white sugarpaste at an angle. Use the remaining white removed from the cake board to model two teardrop shapes for Tom's muzzle. Stick these in position either side of the mouth area and smooth the point of each teardrop into the surface until the join is removed. Mark whiskers using the tip of a cocktail stick. For Tom's paws, split 60g (2oz) of white sugarpaste in half and model three teardrop shapes from each. Stick these together to create the paws.

9 To give expression to Tom's eyes, split 7g (¼oz) of the grey sugarpaste in half and model two long teardrop shapes. For his cheeks, split another 30g (1oz) of the grey sugarpaste in half and model two rounded teardrop shapes. Stick these in position with the rounded end edging the muzzle and eye. Moisten the points of the teardrops and then smooth these into the cake surface, until the join is removed.

10 Colour 125g (4oz) of the modelling paste grey and 45g (1½oz) pink. Using the step photograph as a guide, split the grey modelling paste in half and model Tom's ears. Using 30g (1oz) of the pink paste, cut pieces to cover the inside of each ear, smoothing to remove the ridge. Stick these in position,

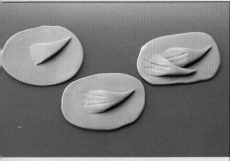

This picture shows you how to create the fur for the sides of Tom's head. Note how the pieces overlap slightly.

Cover the mallet with sugarpaste. First cover the ends and then roll sugarpaste around the whole of the cylinder.

Here are all the basic components to make up Jerry's body.

holding them for a few moments until they are set, or alternatively use pieces of foam sponge to support them until dry.

11 With the remaining grey sugarpaste, model different-sized teardrop shapes, pressing each flat. Stick these in place around the sides of Tom's head, overlapping some of them to build up the impression of fur. Smooth the full end of each piece into the cake surface to remove the join as before. Mark lines on the surface using the back of a knife. Model two teardrop shapes for his 'hair' on top of his head. Using 15g (½oz) of the black modelling paste, shape two eyebrows and his nose. Stick all of these into position.

12 Colour 15g (½oz) of the modelling paste pale golden brown using brown with a touch of orange. Roll just over half into a sausage for the mallet handle and scratch lines into it with a cocktail stick to mark a wood grain effect.

13 Colour the remaining sugarpaste pale golden brown as in step 12. Roll out 60g (2oz), add a little more buttercream to one end of the mallet and position the mallet down onto the paste and cut around it so that the mallet is neatly covered. Cover the opposite end of the mallet in the same way. Roll out the remaining pale golden brown sugarpaste and cut a strip the depth of the mallet, measuring 23cm (9in) in length. Dust it with icing (confectioner's) sugar and roll it up. Add a little more buttercream to the sides of the mallet then position the strip of sugarpaste against the sides and unroll, trimming any excess from the join and smoothing it until closed. Moisten the join around the wide end of the mallet with sugar glue and smooth it closed.

14 Moisten the top of Tom's head with sugar glue. Position the narrower end of the mallet on top of Tom's head, keeping it straight. Still supporting the mallet, push the dowelling through the mallet into Tom's head. Make a small hole in the side of the mallet and stick the handle in. Use a foam piece for support while drying. Scratch the surface of the mallet with a cocktail stick.

TO MAKE JERRY

15 Colour 140g (4½oz) of the modelling paste deep golden brown using brown and orange food colouring paste. Model a ball-shaped head using 75g (2½oz) of the paste and a teardrop-shaped body with 22g (¾oz) of it. Stick the body and head in place on top of the mallet, using a foam piece to support Jerry's head at the chin area.

16 To make Jerry's muzzle, first press a tiny flattened piece of black modelling paste onto the mouth area to create the shadow. Colour a minute amount of modelling paste red and shape a flattened ball to make his tongue. Using the remaining pale golden brown modelling paste, roll a sausage shape, rolling more in the centre to narrow, and round off each end. Stick this onto Jerry's face, outlining the mouth and making a 'v' shape. Model two teardrop shapes for the muzzle and smooth into place. Mark holes with a cocktail stick.

17 With pea-sized amounts of white modelling paste, shape two ovals for Jerry's eyes and stick them in place. Edge each eye with a teardrop shape made from a pea-sized amount of deep golden brown paste.

18 For Jerry's ears, split 15g (½oz) of the deep golden brown in half and shape semicircles. Press them flat, indenting them in the centre and creating a thicker ridge at the front of each. Using the remaining pink modelling paste, fill each ear with a flattened piece of pink. Stick the ears in place and hold them for a few moments until secure.

19 For Jerry's arms, split just under 7g (¼oz) of the deep golden brown modelling paste in half. To make one arm, roll a sausage and round it off at one end. Then make cuts into the rounded end to separate the thumb and fingers. Make the thumb cut slightly to one side then make two cuts across the top, following the curve to make fingers that are full at the ends. Pinch them gently to round them off, and then pinch all the way around the bottom end to shape the wrist. Pinch the arm halfway down to form the elbow and stick the finished arm in position. Make the other arm in the same way. When you position this arm, cross it over the other arm, and tuck the hand under Jerry's chin.

Once Jerry's legs have been positioned, create footpads out of pale brown paste.

20 To make Jerry's legs, split 7g (¼oz) of the deep golden brown modelling paste in half. Roll one piece into a sausage, rounding off one end. Pinch the rounded end to flatten it slightly and gently bend it round. Pinch in to create the heel and then pinch all the way round the leg to shape the ankle. Make one cut at the toe area to separate two toes and smooth to remove ridges. Pinch the leg halfway up to mark the knee and pinch in at the back to bend the leg. Stick this leg in position with sugar glue and then make the second leg as before, sticking it in place in a cross-legged position.

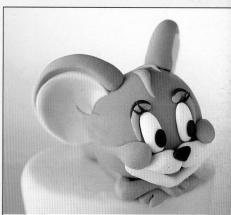

21 With the remaining deep golden brown modelling paste, make the 'hair' and fur pieces for Jerry in the same way as you did for Tom. Then roll a tiny sausage that tapers gently at the tip to form Jerry's tail and stick it in place. With the remaining pale brown paste, model two tiny footpads and then stick them onto the bottom of each foot.

Model Jerry's eyes, eyelashes, eyebrows and nose from black sugarpaste.

22 Using the remaining black modelling paste, model two eyes, four tiny eyelashes, two eyebrows and a nose for Jerry. Use the glue brush to pick up the eyelashes and help stick them in position.

FINISHING TOUCHES

23 Colour the remaining modelling paste bright yellow. Roll out and cut star shapes using the cutter and then stick them in place so that they 'swirl' around Tom's head.

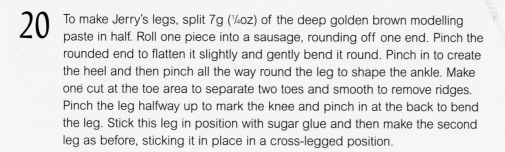

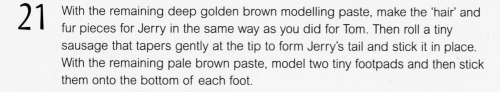

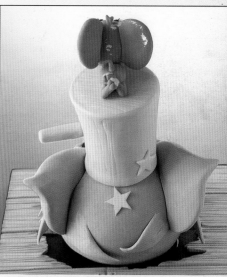

Cut out star shapes and place them around Tom's head.

YŌGI BEAR™

The picnickers in Jellystone Park are just too much of a temptation for Yogi Bear and Boo Boo. Before the visitors know what's happened, their baskets are whisked away from right under their noses!

CAKE AND DECORATION

20cm (8in) square cake (see p.11)

30cm (12in) oval-shaped cake board

1.3kg (2lb 10oz) sugarpaste (rolled fondant)

345g (11oz/1½ cups) buttercream

Black, green, brown, cream, blue and dark red food colouring pastes

Icing (confectioner's) sugar in a sugar shaker

Sugar glue

410g (13oz) modelling paste

EQUIPMENT

Large and small rolling pins

Small knife

Serrated single curve crimping tool

Small brush for sugar glue

Miniature circle cutter

Templates (see p.94)

A few cocktail sticks (toothpicks)

TIME SAVING TIP

Make Yogi alone in the ranger and decorate the basket cake by folding sugarpaste around it to look like a tied tablecloth. Sausages could then be spilling out of an opening in the cloth.

CAKE BOARD AND CAKE

1 Roll out 410g (13oz) of the sugarpaste (rolled fondant) and cover the cake board completely, trimming away any excess. Decorate around the edge by pinching gently with the crimping tool, then put it aside to dry.

2 Trim the crust from the cake and slice the top flat. Cut the cake exactly in half. One half will be the base of the ranger. Cut an 8cm (3in) strip from the second half to form the front and trim one side of it to slope downwards. For the back, cut a 6cm (2½in) strip and trim it to slope downwards as before. Slice this in half to reduce its height. From the remaining cake trim a small oblong shape for the picnic basket, cutting it narrower towards the base to create sloping sides.

3 Sandwich the layers together with buttercream, then spread a thin layer over the surface of the cake to help the sugarpaste stick. Place the ranger cake on the centre of the cake board and put the picnic basket cake aside for later.

THE RANGER

4 Colour.100g (3½oz) of the sugarpaste black. Thinly roll out and cut a strip 56 x 4cm (22 x 1½in) to cover around the base of the cake. Dust this with icing (confectioner's) sugar to prevent it sticking and then roll it up from one end. Put it in place and then unroll it around the base of the cake, trimming excess and smoothing the join closed.

The ranger's base is made from half of the cake. Cut the remaining half to create the front, back and basket.

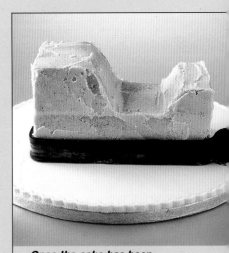
Once the cake has been covered in buttercream, thinly roll out and cut a black strip to cover around the base.

Make the ranger's seat out of brown paste and then model grey wheels.

To mark the criss-cross pattern on the grille press lightly so not to cut the paste.

Cut out cream paste to cover slightly higher than the sides of the picnic basket, marking it all with criss-cross patterns.

5 Colour 410g (13oz) of the sugarpaste dark green using green food colouring paste with a touch of black. Roll out and cover the whole of the ranger, smoothing around the shape. Trim away the excess from around the base to reveal the black strip underneath.

6 Colour 90g (3oz) of the sugarpaste dark brown. Roll out and cut two thick oblong shapes, one measuring 4 x 10cm (1½ x 4in) for the seat back and the other 2.5 x 10cm (1 x 4in) for the seat itself. Stick the seat back in place first, smoothing it around, and then the seat.

7 Colour 185g (6oz) of the sugarpaste dark grey. Split this into four pieces and shape them into flattened circles to make the wheels. Stick them in place with a little sugar glue, making sure that the back two wheels overlap the back and stick out a fraction.

8 Colour 75g (2½oz) of the modelling paste dark green. Roll out 15g (½oz) of this and cut an oblong measuring 8 x 2.5cm (3½ x 1in). To make the windscreen, cut out the inside to make a frame and then put it aside to dry. Measure along the top of the ranger and press in each side to create an indent for the windscreen to slot into later.

9 To make the steering wheel, first colour 15g (½oz) of the modelling paste black. Roll half of it into a ball and press it flat. Cut out circles around the edge using the miniature circle cutter. Stick a small, flattened ball on the centre then put it aside to dry.

10 To decorate the ranger use 60g (2oz) of the dark green modelling paste. Roll out and cut two long strips to edge along the sides, sticking them above each wheel. Roll out and cut two more slightly thinner strips and stick them along the bottom of the previous strips.

11 Thinly roll out and cut an oblong for the front grille using dark green trimmings and mark a criss-cross pattern on it with a knife, pressing gently so the knife does not cut through the paste. Cut two more thin strips to edge the grille at the top and bottom. Cut a long strip to edge the windscreen area and trim a further strip into a point at one end to go on the top of the bonnet. Model two flattened circles for side lights.

12 Colour 30g (1oz) of the modelling paste pale grey using a touch of black food colouring paste. Roll out and cut two bumpers, each slightly wider at either end, and stick in position. Cut two steps, marking a criss-cross pattern as before. Model six balls and press each flat, and then stick two on the front of the ranger for lights. Use the remaining four for the hubcaps.

PICNIC BASKET

13 Thinly roll out the black sugarpaste trimmings and cover the top of the picnic basket cake. If the buttercream has dried, re-work it a little or apply some more. Colour the remaining sugarpaste cream. Roll out and cut pieces to cover the two longest sides of the basket first, making them slightly higher than the sides of the cake. Mark a criss-cross pattern before positioning against the cake sides. Cut two pieces to cover the ends and decorate them in the same way, using sugar glue to secure each corner.

14 For the handle, colour 7g (¼oz) of the modelling paste cream. Roll out and cut a thin strip measuring 9cm (3½in). Bend each end round and put it aside. With the cream trimmings model the apple cores, pinching to create uneven surfaces that resemble bite marks, then put them aside. Colour 45g (1½oz) of the modelling paste light brown. Roll out 7g (¼oz) and cut a strip for the top of the picnic basket.

YOGI BEAR

15 Colour 140g (4½oz) of the modelling paste brown. Using 100g (3½oz), model Yogi's long, teardrop-shaped body. Slightly smooth his back to indent it, which will also push out his tummy, and press the neck area flat. Using 22g (¾oz) shape his head, cutting the top flat, and put it all aside to set.

16 Model a flattened circle for his collar using just under 7g (¼oz) of the white modelling paste and indent at the front using the tip of a knife. Stick Yogi's body into the ranger with his collar on top, making sure the figure sits straight and is well balanced. Stick a small ball of black modelling paste onto the back of the steering wheel and then stick the wheel into position.

17 Split 7g (¼oz) of the brown modelling paste in half and use this for Yogi's two legs. Roll the first one into a sausage shape that is slightly narrower at one end. Bend the narrow end round to shape a foot, pinching it gently to mark a heel. Mark twice at the toe area using the tip of a knife. Bend the full end round and press it flat, then stick the leg in place. Make the second leg.

18 For his arms, split 7g (¼oz) of the brown modelling paste in half. Roll one half into a long sausage shape, slightly narrower at one end. Pinch around the narrow end to create a wrist that then rounds off a small hand. Make a cut, slightly to one side of the hand for the thumb, and then make two more cuts along the top to separate the fingers. Smooth each finger gently to lengthen it. Press in halfway up the arm and pinch out at the back to mark the elbow. Then stick it in place with the hand resting on the steering wheel. Make the second arm in the same way.

19 For Yogi's muzzle, first colour just over 7g (¼oz) of the modelling paste dark cream. Split it almost in half, so that one bit is slightly larger than the other. Put the smaller piece aside for Boo Boo later. Using the larger half and the template (see p.94), shape the mouth area and separate muzzle and stick both in place. Smooth out the join using your finger, rubbing gently with icing (confectioner's) sugar at the sides only. Mark dimples with the miniature circle cutter pressed in at an angle. Indent the muzzle down the centre using a knife, then mark whiskers using the tip of a cocktail stick (toothpick).

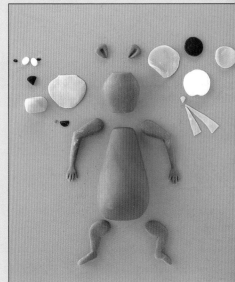

Here are all the components that you need to build up Yogi Bear.

This shows Yogi in position. The steering wheel was stuck in place after his body but before his arms.

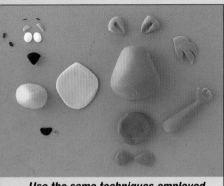

Use the same techniques employed to make each part of Yogi when making Boo Boo.

Model white bread slices for the basket with a little green paste as the filling.

Model the sausages and trail some down the back of the ranger.

20 Press a tiny ball of black modelling paste to make it as thin as possible and shape it into Yogi's smile. Indent gently at his mouth area and then stick on his smile. Stick his head in place and then model two oval-shaped eyes using white paste. Make two black pupils and a triangular-shaped nose.

21 Colour just under 7g (¼oz) of the modelling paste pale green. Using half, model a flattened oval shape, turning it up at each end and stick it in place for Yogi's hat rim. Model a small, flattened circle of black paste and stick this onto his hat for the hat band. Set aside one third of the remaining pale green, then use the larger amount to shape another flattened circle for the top of his hat, press down in the centre and stick it in place. Roll out the rest of the pale green, cut two long triangular shapes and stick these in place for his tie with a small, flattened ball at the indentation of his collar.

22 Using the remaining brown modelling paste, model his two teardrop-shaped ears. Press in the centre of each using the end of a paintbrush and stick them in place. Press gently at each full end to make them more angular.

BOO BOO

23 Press a 7g (¼oz) ball of the light brown modelling paste onto the centre of the basket for Boo Boo's body. Make his arm in the same way as you made Yogi's, but a little shorter. Stick the arm resting against the inside of the picnic basket. For his head, model the shape in the same way as you did Yogi's, but make it slightly fuller at the cheek area and keep the top of his head rounded.

24 Make his facial features like Yogi's (see page 94 for mouth template), but ensure his muzzle is shorter and rounder and his smile smaller. Model tiny light brown eyelids for his eyes. To make his eyebrows, roll a minute piece of black paste into a sausage shape, tapering it at either end, and then cut it in half. Cut his hair from a small, flattened teardrop shape. Make his ears as Yogi's. Colour 7g (¼oz) of the modelling paste bright blue. Model his collar and two triangular pieces for the bow tie. Assemble Boo Boo in the basket.

FINISHING TOUCHES

25 To make the sandwiches, model white sliced bread shapes and stick these together with thin pieces of pale green trimmings. Thinly roll out more white modelling paste and cut a square for the tablecloth filling the picnic basket.

26 Colour 7g (¼oz) of the modelling paste dark red. Thinly roll out and cut squares to decorate a chequered pattern on the tablecloth. Also stick a minute dark red tongue on each of the bears' smiles. Model two dark red rear lights for the ranger. Stick a small dark red flattened circle onto each end of the apple cores and indent their centres with a cocktail stick.

27 Colour the remaining modelling paste reddish brown using a little dark red and brown food colouring pastes and model all the sausages. Arrange the sausages in the picnic basket with some trailing down the back of the ranger. When the cake is dry, slot in the windscreen using sugar glue, and stick the basket handle in place fully forwards, supported by the tablecloth.

TOP CAT ™

With his great friend Benny standing guard, perhaps this time Top Cat will actually get away with using Officer Dibble's telephone without getting caught…

CAKE AND DECORATION

2 x 15cm (6in) round cakes (see p.11)

35 x 25cm (14 x 10in) oblong cake board

1.3kg (2lb 10oz) sugarpaste (rolled fondant)

Blue, black, yellow, purple, mauve, cream and brown food colouring pastes

1.115kg (2lb 4¼oz) modelling paste

Icing (confectioner's) sugar in a sugar shaker

Sugar glue

345g (11oz/1½ cups) buttercream

Edible silver dusting powder (petal dust/blossom tint)

EQUIPMENT

Large and small rolling pins

Sharp knife

15cm (6in) diameter shallow bowl

Small glue brush

Small piece of foam sponge and foam sheet

Soft dusting brush

Templates (see p.94)

Cocktail sticks (toothpicks)

Fine paintbrush

CAKE BOARD AND CAKE

1 Colour 440g (14oz) of the sugarpaste (rolled fondant) pale blue/grey using a touch each of blue and black food colouring pastes. Roll out and cover the cake board completely. Roll the surface gently with the large rolling pin pressing into the surface randomly to create ripples. Trim excess from around the edge, smooth the ridge and then put it aside to dry.

2 Colour 410g (13oz) of the modelling paste grey. Dust the outside of the shallow bowl with icing (confectioner's) sugar. This will be the mould for the trash can lid. Roll out 170g (5½oz) of the paste and position it over the bowl, smoothing it around the shape. To make the indented pattern around the edge, press in gently with your finger. Check that the paste has not actually stuck to the bowl as you need to be able to remove it later, then trim away the excess from around the edge.

3 Roll out 75g (2½oz) of the grey modelling paste and cut a 2 x 50cm (¾ x 20in) strip. Moisten the edge of the trash can lid with sugar glue and carefully stick the strip in place. Trim the excess at the join and smooth closed.

4 Using 30g (1oz) of the grey paste, roll out and cut another strip measuring 15cm (6in) in length. Bend each end round, pinching them up slightly, and stick the piece onto the top of the trash can lid to make the handle. If necessary, use a piece of foam sponge to

A shallow bowl is used to form the shape required for the trash can lid.

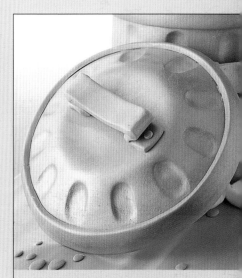

The trash can lid handle is made by bending and pinching a strip of grey modelling paste.

39

Unroll the grey sugarpaste around the cake to make the trash can.

Use a brush to apply edible silver dusting powder in awkward areas.

Build up Top Cat on top of the trash can, positioning his body nearer one side so that his elbow rests on the rim.

support the centre until dry. Model two flattened balls using trimmings and stick them in place at either end of the handle using sugar glue. Leave the lid to dry completely on the bowl before removing it.

5 Trim the crust from each cake and slice the tops flat where they have risen. Sandwich the two cakes together with buttercream, then spread a thin layer of buttercream over the surface of the cakes to help the sugarpaste stick.

6 Colour 625g (1¼lb) of the sugarpaste grey using a little black food colouring paste. Roll it out and cut a piece to cover the side of the cake, measuring 50cm (20in) in length. Dust the surface of the sugarpaste with icing (confectioner's) sugar, then roll it up at either end so that the rolls meet in the centre. Carefully pick the paste up then position it against the cake. Unroll the sugarpaste around the cake and cut away any excess at the join. Press the join together, sticking with a little sugar glue, then rub it closed. To indent the pattern, press evenly around the sides using the small rolling pin.

7 Colour 75g (2½oz) of the sugarpaste black. Thinly roll this out and cover the top of the cake, trimming away any excess from around the edge. Using 75g (2½oz) of the grey modelling paste, roll out and cut a strip measuring 2.5 x 50cm (1 x 20in) and use it to edge the top, leaving about half of the depth above the top of the cake. With the remaining grey, make two more handles as before and stick them on opposite sides of the trash can.

8 To make the small food tin lying on the cake board using grey trimmings, model a sausage shape and cut the two ends straight. Mark indented lines all the way around the tin using the back of a knife, and then make small ragged cuts around the top edge. Roll out and cut a circle for the open lid, again cutting the edge ragged, and then put it all aside to dry.

9 Apply the edible silver dusting powder (petal dust/blossom tint) to the trash can and lid and the small food tin using your fingers to rub gently in a circular motion. Use a soft dusting brush to apply the colour in awkward areas. Carefully lift the cake and position it on the cake board as quickly as possible to prevent marks. Stick the small food can in place, slightly to one side, leaving room for Benny.

TOP CAT AND HIS PILLOW

10 Using 170g (5½oz) of the white sugarpaste, roll an oval shape and pinch up four corners to make Top Cat's pillow. Stick it in position on the top edge of the trash can, half supported by the inside of the can, and then indent it in the centre to create a dip for Top Cat's head.

11 Colour 355g (11½oz) of the modelling paste yellow. Using 125g (4oz), model a teardrop shape for his body. Flatten the point of the teardrop, and then stick it in position on top of the trash can, slightly off centre.

12 Split 30g (1oz) of yellow in half and use it to make his two arms. First, roll one into a sausage shape with a rounded end. Press the rounded end flatter, then make a cut slightly to one side for the thumb. Make two more

Form Top Cat's head and rest it on the pillow. Then make fur pieces before modelling the waistcoat.

The top of the receiver should be positioned level with Top Cat's eyes.

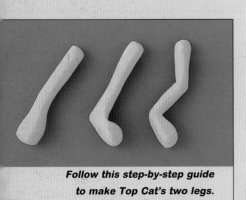

Follow this step-by-step guide to make Top Cat's two legs.

cuts along the top to separate the fingers. Gently pinch to shape and round them off. Pinch halfway up the arm to mark the elbow and then stick it in position. Make the opposite arm in the same way, but reverse the thumb cut and stick it in place, leaving room for the telephone receiver.

13 Colour 45g (1½oz) of the modelling paste purple. Using 15g (½oz), thinly roll out and cut two waistcoat pieces using the template (see p.94). Position and add three small, flattened circles for buttons down the centre.

14 Roll 125g (4oz) of the yellow modelling paste into a ball for his head and stick it in place so that it rests on the pillow. Cut off the top of his head to create a flat area for the hat to sit on. For the fur either side of his face, model two small and two slightly larger teardrop shapes. Press each flat and cut away the full ends at an angle so each will sit neatly against opposite sides of his head. Moisten them with sugar glue and stick each into position. To remove the joins, smooth into the surface of the head using a little sugar glue on your finger, then rub gently with icing (confectioner's) sugar. Gently stroke each tip so that it curls upwards.

15 Using 15g (½oz) of the white modelling paste, shape the muzzle (see p.94) and stick it onto his face leaving room for his eyes. Then model a ball and stick it onto the muzzle, smoothing into the surface either side to remove the join. Mark down the centre using a knife and indent whiskers using the tip of a cocktail stick (toothpick). Indent dimples either side to create his cheeky smile and model two oval-shaped eyes.

16 Using 15g (½oz) of the purple modelling paste, model a flattened circle to make the hat rim. Colour 45g (1½oz) of the modelling paste black and shape a thicker flattened circle using 15g (½oz) to make the hat band. Shape the remaining purple modelling paste into a flattened circle and pinch up a top ridge, smoothing a small indentation in the top. Stick this onto the band, then stick the completed hat onto his head.

17 Flatten a tiny piece of black modelling paste and shape his mouth area and make his nose and two pupils. Stick these all in place. Model two small, pointed ears using a pea-sized amount of yellow for each and stick in position on the hat rim, slightly leaning forward. To make the telephone receiver, roll 15g (½oz) of the black modelling paste into a sausage shape, rounding off both ends. Bend each end around and stick into Top Cat's hand.

18 To make his legs, split 60g (2oz) of the yellow modelling paste in half. Roll one half into a sausage shape, rounding off one end. Bend this end round for the foot and pinch it gently to shape the heel. Press either side to shape the foot and make three cuts along the top to create toes. Pinch halfway up the leg to shape the knee and pinch in at the back to bend a little, then stick in place. Make the second leg, crossing it over the other leg.

19 For his tail, roll 15g (½oz) of the yellow modelling paste into a sausage, slightly thicker at one end, and stick it in place, curling up at the end. Use the remaining yellow to make the banana skin. Model it into a sausage shape that tapers at both ends. Make a cut that goes two-thirds of the way down the centre, leaving a third of it uncut at one end. Open the cut up and cut into each resulting piece down the middle to make four sections. Pinch up an edge along the top of each section and then bend them into position. Set the banana skin aside for later.

BENNY

20 Colour 200g (6½oz) of the modelling paste mauve. Benny is modelled flat, then placed on a foam sheet to dry completely before being positioned against the cake. Model his body first, using 60g (2oz) of the mauve paste. To make his feet, split 22g (¾oz) of the mauve in half and make his feet in the same way as you did Top Cat's, but make the legs much shorter.

21 For his head, roll a ball using 90g (3oz) of the mauve modelling paste and stick it onto the body. Using 7g (¼oz) of the mauve, make his ears as you did Top Cat's, but make them slightly wider. Also model four fur pieces, smoothing them into the sides of his face.

22 Using 7g (¼oz) of the white modelling paste, roll out and cut his waistcoat using the template (see p.94). Stick this in place and add a small, flattened circle as a button. To make his arms, split the remaining mauve in half. Model the arms as you did for Top Cat's, but make them much shorter and do not indent elbows into them. Keep them a little fuller at the shoulder. To help stick each arm securely, make two small indents at each side of his body using your finger. Then stick the arms in each recess, positioning them and sticking them against his head for extra support.

The components for Benny are on the right, facial details and waistcoat to the left.

23 Colour 22g (¾oz) of the modelling paste flesh using cream with a tiny amount of dark red. To make Benny's face, model a flattened circle for his eye area, and then make his inner ears. Use the template to make his muzzle.

24 With the remaining black modelling paste, make Benny's eyes, eyebrows, nose and mouth area and stick all in place. Also stick a flattened circle onto the small food tin. With the blue/grey sugarpaste trimmings, model flattened oval shapes for pebbles and stick them randomly over the surface of the cake board, and then model the fish head and tail.

FINISHING TOUCHES

25 To make the fish bone, thinly roll out 7g (¼oz) of the white modelling paste and cut a long strip for the backbone, and then small strips of various lengths. Assemble the fish bone with the slightly longer strips at the centre. Thinly roll out the remaining white paste and cut oblong shapes for the newspaper and arrange it all around Top Cat.

26 When the cake is dry, stick Benny in place, holding him until he is secure. Then position the trash can lid, resting it against the trash can for support. Dilute a little brown food colouring paste with a drop of water. Using the fine paintbrush paint the banana and then stick it in place. Dilute some black colouring paste and lightly paint scribbled lines to resemble newsprint.

Model the finishing touches and stick Benny in place against the trash can.

THE POWERPUFF GIRLS ™

These pint-sized Powerpuff Girls are the cutest crime-busting super heroes you'll ever see. Having saved the world, here they are having a playful pillow fight before bedtime.

CAKE AND DECORATION

20cm (8in) square cake (see p.11)

35cm (14in) round cake board

1.57kg (3lb 3oz) sugarpaste (rolled fondant)

Pink, blue, green, golden brown, black, yellow and red food colouring pastes

Icing (confectioner's) sugar in a sugar shaker

720g (1lb 7oz) modelling paste

220g (7oz) buttercream

Sugar glue

Five 5cm (2in) sugar sticks or lengths of raw, dried spaghetti

EQUIPMENT

Large and small rolling pins

Small knife

Templates (see p.93)

Foam sheet

Small brush for sugar glue

5cm (2in), 2.5cm (1in), 2cm (¾in), 1.5cm (½in) and miniature circle cutters

Ruler

Small pieces of foam sponge to aid drying

Various small star cutters

CUTTING AND COVERING THE CAKE

1 Colour 500g (1lb) of the sugarpaste (rolled fondant) pale pink, roll it out and cover the cake board. Colour 280g (9oz) of the modelling paste pink. Using the template (see p.93), roll out and cut the headboard and place it on the foam sheet to dry.

2 Slice the top from the cake where the cake has risen, then trim off the crust. Turn the cake upside down. Cut a 4.5cm (1¾in) slice from one side of the cake and cut two squares from this strip for the bedside tables. Trim the corners from each of these in order to make them round.

3 To shape the bed, trim the top and bottom edge from opposite sides and at the end only. Split and fill the two bedside tables with buttercream, then spread a layer of buttercream over all the cakes to help the sugarpaste stick.

4 Colour 625g (1¼lb) of the sugarpaste pink. Roll it out and cover the large cake, trimming the excess and smoothing round the shape. Position the cake on the centre of the board.

5 Colour 170g (5½oz) of the sugarpaste purple using pink with a touch of blue food colouring paste. Roll out 75g (2½oz) and cut a strip the depth of a bedside table. Position one of the tables onto this strip and cover it, trimming any excess before smoothing the join with your

Cut and shape the small cakes into the two bedside tables.

Roll out purple sugarpaste and use it to cover the bedside tables with.

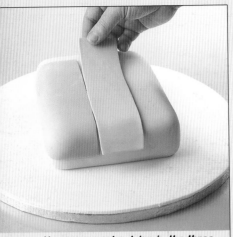

fingers. Using the back of a knife, mark vertical lines on either side of the bedside table, then a horizontal line to mark two drawers. Use trimmings to model two handles and stick them on with a little sugar glue. Cover the second bedside table in the same way. To cover the top of each, use pink sugarpaste trimmings and cut two circles using the 5cm (2in) circle cutter. Position and smooth the top edge.

6 With the remaining purple sugarpaste, thinly roll out and cut a heart using the template (see p.93). Stick it onto the headboard using a little sugar glue and smooth to remove the ridge around the edge.

Use sugarpaste strips in the three colours to create the bedcover.

MODELLING THE ACCESSORIES

7 To make the striped bedcover, colour 100g (3½oz) of the sugarpaste green, 75g (2½oz) deep pink and 100g (3½oz) blue. Roll out the green and cut a strip to cover one third of the bed, leaving a gap at the top and base. Smooth at the base to give a 'tucked in' appearance. Complete the bedcover with deep pink and blue stripes.

8 Split 90g (3oz) of the white modelling paste into three pieces. To make a pillow, shape into an oval and pinch up four corners. Bend into position and stick onto the headboard. Make two more pillows and position them on the bed. Push sugar sticks or lengths of raw, dried spaghetti through these, leaving the sticks protruding.

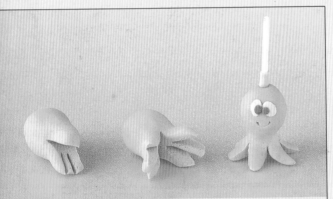

Make the octopus lamp base by cutting legs from an oval shape. Finish by placing a sugar stick in the top.

9 Colour 22g (¾oz) of the modelling paste deep pink. Using just under 7g (¼oz) to make the teddy lamp base, model an oval-shaped body and head. Stick the head securely to the body then shape two small ears. With some pale pink trimmings, model a flattened circle for his tummy patch, a muzzle and two eyes. Mark a smile using the miniature circle cutter pushed in at an upwards angle and shape four tiny sausages of deep pink to stick onto his body for paws. Push a sugar stick through his body, leaving it protruding in order to hold the lampshade in place after it is made.

10 To make the octopus lamp base, roll 7g (¼oz) of deep pink modelling paste into an oval. Pinch in the middle to create the neck. Make cuts to separate the legs, mark a smile and make two eyes using pale and deep pink trimmings. Push a sugar stick down through the octopus. Using a little deep pink paste, wrap a piece around the base of each sugar stick, just above the top of each lamp base.

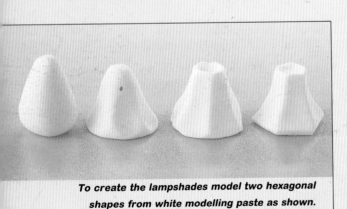

To create the lampshades model two hexagonal shapes from white modelling paste as shown.

11 To make the lampshades, split 60g (2oz) of white modelling paste in half. Shape one piece into a teardrop and press the rounded end down to flatten it.

Pinch all the way around to make a hexagonal shape and then press the top of the lampshade to indent it. Neaten the base of the shade using a knife. Make the second lampshade in the same way, then push them both onto the sugar sticks in each lamp base to check the fit. Remove them and allow to dry completely before assembling.

MAKING THE POWERPUFF GIRLS

12 Colour 140g (4½oz) of the modelling paste flesh-coloured using golden brown and pink food colouring pastes. Put aside 7g (¼oz), then split the rest into three equal pieces and model oval heads with smiles. Stick one onto the headboard, leaving room for the body when the headboard is positioned.

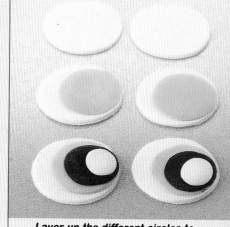

Layer up the different circles to create the girls' eyes.

13 Colour 22g (¾oz) of the modelling paste black, and just under 7g (¼oz) each of blue and green. Using the circle cutters, sizes 2.5cm (1in) down to miniature, and the very thinly rolled out white, blue, green, deep pink and black modelling paste, make all the eyes. Use sugar glue and push the remaining two heads onto the sugar sticks in each pillow. Place pieces of foam under them for support while drying.

14 Model the girls' nightdresses using the rest of the blue, green and deep pink modelling pastes, pinching an edge around each base, and stick them in position. Model six teardrop-shaped arms and legs using the remaining flesh-coloured modelling paste. Model small flattened balls of white modelling paste. Cut each in half and use to edge the nightdresses.

15 Colour 22g (¾oz) of the modelling paste golden brown. Using Blossom's hair template (see p.93), roll out the golden brown paste and cut out her hair shapes. Stick the top part onto her head, smoothing around the back. Stick the second piece onto the headboard.

Smooth the bottom of Buttercup's hair to curl it upwards.

16 Colour 30g (1oz) of the modelling paste yellow. Take half and follow Bubbles' hair template (see p.93) to cut out her hair. Stick it in place and model her bunches. Roll out the rest of the black modelling paste and cut out Buttercup's hair using the template (see p.93). Stick it in place and smooth the end, curling it upwards.

FINISHING TOUCHES

17 Colour 7g (¼oz) of the modelling paste purple. To make the bunny, model half of this paste into an oval-shaped head (see the picture on the right as a guide). With the rest, make two long ears and a flattened ball for the body. Use small cuts to make arms and legs, and mark a little cross for the mouth. Make eyes with black and white modelling paste trimmings.

18 Colour the rest of the modelling paste deep red. Model Blossom's hair bow, the eyes and noses on the lamp bases and the bunny's tail. Stick the headboard in place. Lastly, thinly roll out the remaining yellow modelling paste and cut out stars to decorate around the cake board edge.

Cut out different-sized stars to decorate the edge of the board.

Dexter needs to watch out because his meddling big sister Dee Dee has entered his laboratory and is just about to cause hysterical mayhem again!

CAKE AND DECORATION

20cm (8in) square cake (see p.11)

25cm (10in) square cake board

875g (1¾lb) sugarpaste (rolled fondant)

Blue, mauve, black, green, yellow, red, pink and cream food colouring pastes

440g (14oz/1¾ cups) buttercream

Sugar glue

250g (8oz) modelling paste

Icing (confectioner's) sugar in a sugar shaker

EQUIPMENT

Large and small rolling pins

Sharp knife

Ruler

Small brush for glue

Medium paintbrush

No.4 plain piping tube (tip)

Piece of foam sponge

2.5cm (1in) circle cutter

Template (see p.93)

TIME SAVING TIP

Make one large computer and indent into the surface of the sugarpaste instead of sticking each of the details on separately.

CAKE BOARD AND CAKE

1 Colour 345g (11oz) of the sugarpaste (rolled fondant) blue. Roll it out and cover the cake board completely, trimming the excess from around the edge. Measure evenly around the cake board and then indent lines with a ruler to create the chequered pattern. Put the cake board aside to dry.

2 Trim the crust from the cake and slice the top flat where the cake has risen. Cut the cake in half and put one half on top of the other. Then trim two small wedges from the top, one slightly deeper than the other. Sandwich the two cake layers together with buttercream, then spread a thin layer of buttercream over the surface of the cake to help the sugarpaste stick. Position the cake on the cake board, towards the back.

THE COMPUTERS

3 Colour 280g (9oz) of the sugarpaste mauve. Roll out 90g (3oz) of mauve and use it to cover the sides of the two mauve computers. (So that the central mauve computer protrudes further than the other computers, roll out the sugarpaste slightly thicker than usual.) Using another 60g (2oz), roll out and cut pieces to cover the back of the computers, then cover the front and finally the top using 100g (3½oz), securing all joins with sugar glue.

4 Colour the remaining sugarpaste pale grey using a touch of black food colouring paste.

Indent lines into the sugarpaste using ruler to create a chequered pattern.

Spread a layer of buttercream over the cake so the sugarpaste will stick.

Cover the two tallest sections of the shape with mauve sugarpaste.

Roll out and cut pieces to cover the two grey computers, covering the side first, then the back and front and finally the top. Secure all the joins closed with sugar glue.

5 Colour 7g (¼oz) of the modelling paste bright green, 30g (1oz) yellow, a tiny piece pale blue and another red. Using a little yellow, all the pale blue, red, and the mauve and grey sugarpaste trimmings, make all the detailing on the front and sides of the computers. The circles can be indented with both ends of the plain piping tube (tip) as shown, while the lines and squares are indented into thinly rolled-out sugarpaste and then cut out. The holes are indented using the end of a paintbrush. Join these holes up using a knife to mark lines. Cut different-sized yellow triangular shapes to edge around the red button.

DEE DEE

6 To make Dee Dee, first colour 125g (4oz) of the modelling paste flesh-coloured using a touch each of the pink and cream food colouring pastes. Using 60g (2oz) of it, model an oval-shaped head and pull gently underneath to make her neck. Stick it in place on the front of the computer and hold it for a few moments until it is secure. If necessary, use a piece of foam sponge for support while it is drying.

7 Colour 15g (½oz) of the modelling paste pink. Model her tiny sausage-shaped body using a bit of the pink and stick this onto the end of her neck. Put aside two pea-sized amounts of pink, then split the remainder in half and model two teardrop-shaped shoes. Stick a small white flattened teardrop onto the top of each.

8 Model two long teardrop-shaped legs using a pea-sized amount of white for each, and stick everything in place with one leg bent up and stuck against the front of the computer in a running pose. Thinly roll out the pea-sized amount of pink paste and cut four tiny strips for her ankle ties. Cut a strip for her skirt and wrap this around the top of her legs, smoothing up around the base using a damp paintbrush.

9 To make her arms, first split 7g (¼oz) of the flesh-coloured modelling paste into three pieces. Put one piece aside. Roll the second piece into a long teardrop shape and press the full end a little flat. Make three cuts to separate fingers and pinch at the tip of each to round them off. Stick the arm in position as soon as it is made, bending the hand and pulling up the index finger so that it looks as if it is about to press the red button. Make the opposite arm in the same way, using the third piece, and stick it against the front of the computer.

10 For her hair, thinly roll out yellow modelling paste and cut two circles using the circle cutter. Stick them onto the top of Dee Dee's head on either side. Split 22g (¾oz) of the yellow in half and model them into her teardrop-shaped bunches, pulling the point of each to curl round.

Model all the detailing for the computers using various colours of modelling paste.

Here are all the pieces that you need to make up Dexter's sister Dee Dee.

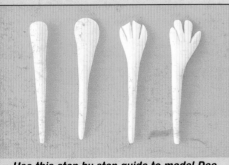

Use this step-by-step guide to model Dee Dee's arms and hands.

11 Thinly roll out a pea-sized amount of white modelling paste and cut out her eyes using the end of the piping tube. Colour a small ball of modelling paste blue. Using half, model Dee Dee's two irises.

12 Colour 15g (½oz) of the modelling paste black. Thinly roll out a pea-sized amount and cut out her smile using the template (see p.93). Stick this in place along with a tiny pink tongue. Model two ears and a pointed nose using flesh-coloured paste.

13 Colour the remaining modelling paste orange using red and yellow food colouring paste. Model the bottle with a little flattened ball for the lid. Colour a pea-sized amount of the modelling paste deep blue for the test tube.

Dee Dee is built up against the computer in a running pose.

DEXTER

14 To make Dexter's shoes, split just under 7g (¼oz) of the black modelling paste in half. Model a teardrop shape first, cut a 'v' in the centre and pinch around the heel to make it angular. Make the second shoe and stick them both together.

15 To make his tunic, roll a fat sausage of white modelling paste using 15g (½oz). Cut the top, slicing at a slight upward angle. Indent the front by pressing in with the back of a knife and then stick this onto the shoes, making sure that the tunic is well balanced. Using white trimmings, stick on two tiny sleeves. Colour a pea-sized amount of the modelling paste mauve and use this for his gloved hands. To make them, follow the method used for Dee Dee's hands, but make sure his fingers are much shorter.

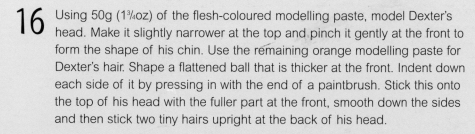

Follow this step-by-step guide to model Dexter.

16 Using 50g (1¾oz) of the flesh-coloured modelling paste, model Dexter's head. Make it slightly narrower at the top and pinch it gently at the front to form the shape of his chin. Use the remaining orange modelling paste for Dexter's hair. Shape a flattened ball that is thicker at the front. Indent down each side of it by pressing in with the end of a paintbrush. Stick this onto the top of his head with the fuller part at the front, smooth down the sides and then stick two tiny hairs upright at the back of his head.

17 For his mouth, stick on a tiny sausage of the left-over flesh modelling paste, bending it up at the corners. Moisten the top with sugar glue, then smooth into the surface of his face to remove the join. For the sides of his mouth, stick on tiny flattened balls and smooth in as before.

18 Model a tiny pointed nose and two ears. To make Dexter's glasses, model two small arms for them and then two flattened circles of black modelling paste. Cut one of these circles in half. Using the remaining blue, make his eyes in the same way. Use black paste again to stick on two black pupils, an eyebrow that looks like a small tick and two tunic buttons. Position Dexter on the cake board, turning him slightly towards Dee Dee.

Position Dexter in front of the computer, looking towards Dee Dee.

JOHNNY BRAVO ™

Image-obsessed and ultra-cool dude Johnny Bravo wants to be a hit with the ladies, but he spends too long looking at himself in the mirror!

CAKE AND DECORATION

2 x 15cm (6in) heart-shaped cakes (see p.11)

35cm (14in) round cake board

1.5kg (3lb) sugarpaste (rolled fondant)

Blue, red, black and cream food colouring pastes

375g (12oz/1½ cups) buttercream

155g (5oz) modelling paste

7.5cm (3in) sugar stick or raw, dried spaghetti

Sugar glue

Icing (confectioner's) sugar in a sugar shaker

Yellow and dark cream dusting powders (petal dust/blossom tint)

EQUIPMENT

Large and small rolling pins

Small knife

Small pieces of foam sponge

Medium and fine paintbrushes

A few cocktail sticks (toothpicks)

Medium brush for glue

Template (see p.93)

CAKE BOARD AND CAKE

1 Colour 500g (1lb) of the sugarpaste (rolled fondant) blue. Roll this out and cover the cake board, trimming excess from around the edge, then put it aside to dry. Trim the crust from both cakes and slice the tops flat.

2 Cut a layer in one cake, making one part twice the depth of the other. Trim around the edge of the deeper layer to make it slightly smaller and then do the same for the shallow layer, making it smaller still. Cut the other cake into two layers and then sandwich it back together with buttercream. This will be the main cake. Spread the surface of all three cakes with buttercream to help the sugarpaste stick.

3 Colour 1kg (2lb) of the sugarpaste red. Roll out 500g (1lb) and cover the large heart cake completely, smoothing around the shape and trimming any excess from around the base. Carefully position this cake on the cake board. Cover the remaining two cakes using 375g (12oz) of the red sugarpaste and arrange them on the cake board. With the remaining red, model different-sized heart shapes and use to decorate around the cakes.

The three heart cakes are made from two, as one cake is cut into two different levels.

To make a decorative heart, model a teardrop shape, use a knife to cut a slit at the top and then smooth either side.

Model Johnny's body, supporting it with a piece of foam sponge.

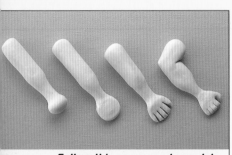

Follow this sequence to model Johnny's two arms. Bend into position and allow to set.

Make the legs by rolling a piece of blue modelling paste into a sausage shape and then cutting it down the middle. Pinch to form each leg and bend one leg over the other.

MAKING JOHNNY

4 Colour 90g (3oz) of the modelling paste black. Put aside just under 7g (¼oz) for later and then, with the remainder, model a large, rounded teardrop shape and place flat down on the worksurface. (The deep colour will have made the modelling paste quite soft, so try not to handle it too much.) Press into the largest end using your finger to open up the neck area of Johnny's t-shirt. Next, push in either side to create small sockets for his arms to slot into. Press the bottom point of the teardrop flat to create his waist area.

5 Johnny's body is quite angular, so pinch and stroke gently to create a ridge around the neck area and down the opposite sides. Leave the piece to set for around ten minutes and then place it on its side, supported by a piece of foam sponge. To round off the back, smooth gently with your fingers. Indent the spine by pressing in with the side of a paintbrush.

6 Colour 45g (1½oz) of the modelling paste a flesh colour using cream food colouring paste with a tiny amount of red. Using 7g (¼oz), shape his angular head, with the facial area tapering down much narrower than the top. The sides of the face and around the chin are extremely angular, so press his face down onto the worksurface to flatten then again either side of his face. Push a cocktail stick (toothpick) into the bottom of his head and then remove it, to make a hole for the sugar stick. Put the head aside to dry.

7 To make the arms, split 22g (¾oz) of the remaining flesh-coloured modelling paste in half. Using half, roll into a sausage shape and taper it so that it is narrower at one end. Round off the narrow end by pinching gently all the way round to create the wrist. Press this rounded end gently to flatten it slightly to form a hand. Make a cut to one side for the thumb and then make three cuts along the top to separate fingers. Next, pinch the arm gently to lengthen it and bend it round. Push in to mark the elbow and pinch out at the back. Bend this arm into position against the body to achieve the correct pose, then remove it and put it to one side to allow it to set. Make the opposite arm in the same way.

8 Split 7g (¼oz) of the flesh-coloured modelling paste in half and use one half to shape Johnny's neck and shoulder area. Press this into the recess at his neck and smooth it so it fits neatly. Secure it with sugar glue. Push the sugar stick down through the neck and body, leaving at least 2.5cm (1in) protruding from the top to help support the head later.

9 Colour just over 7g (¼oz) of the modelling paste blue. Put a pea-sized amount of this aside, and then use the rest of it to make the trousers. First, roll the paste into a long, teardrop shape and make a cut to separate the two legs. Mark the knees by pinching halfway up and push in at the back. Bend one leg up to rest on the other and then press the top of the legs straight at the waist and stick them in place against Johnny's body, smoothing the top and trousers together securely. Use the piece that was set aside earlier to make Johnny's trouser turn-ups.

OH DOUBLE MAMA™

10 With pea-sized amounts of black modelling paste, make the shoes. To make each one, start with a teardrop shape then cut a small 'v' from one side at the rounded end to make a heel. Pinch gently at the back of the heel to straighten it, and then slightly turn up the toe area at the point.

Make Johnny's shoes, cutting a small 'v' for the heel.

11 Using just over 7g (¼oz) of the flesh-coloured modelling paste, make the hair. Follow the step photograph as a modelling guide. Cut three times into the top to make quiffs and press each one gently to round it off. The second quiff is longer than the rest, so gently stroke it upwards to lengthen it.

12 Check that the base of the hair is a fraction larger than the top of Johnny's head before you moisten with sugar glue and stick it securely in place. Smooth the excess down around his head and rub it gently to remove the join. If the paste is dry and cracked, moisten it with sugar glue. It will also help if you dampen your hands slightly as you work. If excess paste builds up on your hands, wipe it away immediately. When the join is closed, rub the surface with a little icing (confectioner's) sugar to remove the join completely.

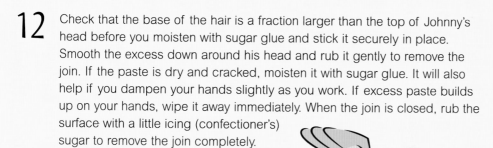

13 Using the yellow dusting powder (petal dust/blossom tint) and the medium paintbrush, colour the hair yellow. Brush on a little at a time, building up the depth of colour and letting it fade around his face. Using sugar glue, secure the arms in position on the t-shirt, and then stick his head in place, pushing down gently over the sugar stick.

Form Johnny's quiff and then colour it yellow using dusting powder.

14 Put a tiny amount of white modelling paste aside for later, then colour the remainder yellow using the yellow dusting powder. Roll out and cut the back piece of the hair using the template (see p.93). Stick this in place around the back of his head, ensuring that the base overlaps the join at the back of the neck to help hide it and hold the head in position more securely.

15 Using the rest of the flesh-coloured modelling paste, model a tiny triangular-shaped nose and stick this onto the centre of his face. Model two tiny oval-shaped ears and indent in the centre of each with the end of a paintbrush. Stick these in place either side of his head, level with his nose. Model a tiny white smile, keeping it as thin as possible, and stick it in place, off centre.

16 With the remaining black modelling paste, make Johnny's capped sleeves by cutting two thin strips that taper at each end and stick them in place. Then model his sunglasses by making two flattened circles and joining them with tiny strips of paste. Mix dark cream dusting powder with icing sugar and then brush this over his skin for a sun-tanned look. Dilute a tiny amount of black food colouring paste with a little water. Using the fine paintbrush, paint a fine line to edge his smile. Finally, stick the figure in position on the centre of the largest heart-shaped cake, holding for a few moments until secure.

Finish modelling the details and then stick Johnny on the largest heart.

COW and CHICKEN ™

This popular cartoon from the Cartoon Network features a fun relationship between a brother and sister. They are unusual siblings – a chicken with attitude and an enormous cow!

CAKE AND DECORATION

20cm (8in) square cake (see p.11)

25cm (10in) round cake board

1.4kg (2lb 12¾oz) sugarpaste (rolled fondant)

Blue, yellow, pink, brown, black and red food colouring pastes

500g (1lb/2 cups) buttercream

Icing (confectioner's) sugar in a sugar shaker

Sugar glue

100g (3½oz) modelling paste

EQUIPMENT

Large rolling pin

Sharp knife

Small brush for glue

Cake smoother

Template (see p.93)

A few cocktail sticks (toothpicks)

Pieces of foam sponge

CAKE BOARD AND CAKE

1 Colour 315g (10oz) of the sugarpaste (rolled fondant) blue. Roll this out and cover the cake board completely, trimming the excess from around the edge, then put it aside to dry.

2 Trim the crust from the cake and slice the top flat where the cake has risen. Cut the cake into four equally sized squares and stack these one on top of the other. To shape Cow's head trim the top of the cake, slicing down and out all the way round, from the top layer down to the next, cutting a deeper wedge at the back.

3 Trim off all corners around the cake to round it off. Sandwich all the layers together using buttercream, then spread a thin layer over the cake's surface to help the sugarpaste stick.

MODELLING COW

4 Colour 875g (1¾lb) of the sugarpaste pale yellow. Roll out 750g (1½lb) and cut an oblong measuring 35cm (14in) in length and 20cm (8in) in height. Dust it liberally with icing (confectioner's) sugar to prevent sticking and roll it up at either end. Position against the front of the cake and then carefully unroll the sugarpaste around it.

5 Smooth the sugarpaste in at the top and trim any excess away at the join. Pinch to close the opening, securing it with sugar glue and leaving a thin join line. With a little icing sugar on your hands, gently rub this join line until it

Stack the four pieces of cake on top of one another and then shape them.

Use icing sugar to smooth the yellow sugarpaste join closed.

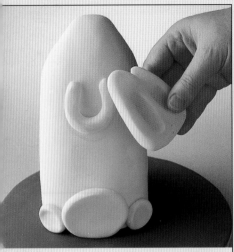

Model the snout then stick it in position, holding for a few moments until secure.

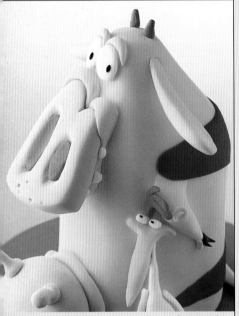

Position the pupils so Cow and Chicken are looking at one another.

Use the template to cut out the two patches for Cow's back.

has been completely removed. Pick the cake up and place it on the cake board, towards the back. If the surface of the sugarpaste is uneven, rub gently in a circular motion using a cake smoother.

6 Roll 22g (¾oz) of the pale yellow sugarpaste into a sausage, tapering it at either end and bending it round. Flatten it slightly and then line it up so that the bottom is in the centre of Cow. Stick it in place using a little sugar glue. Model a flattened circle using another 30g (1oz) of the pale yellow and stick this onto the base of Cow at the front. Model two more flattened circles using another 15g (½oz) and stick these either side.

7 Colour 200g (6½oz) of the sugarpaste pale pink. Using the template (see p.93) and 75g (2½oz) of the paste, thickly roll out and cut the snout shape. Smooth around it to remove any ridges. Indent two nostrils, one longer than the other, using your finger. Mark holes at the bottom with a cocktail stick (toothpick). Stick the snout in place, holding until it is secure.

8 For the top of the snout, split 7g (¼oz) of the pale yellow sugarpaste into two pieces, one larger than the other. Model sausages that taper at each end and use them to edge the top of the snout. Smooth in at the sides to remove the joins.

9 Using white modelling paste, make two eyes, one slightly larger than the other, and edge the top of each with pale yellow sausages that taper at each end. For teeth, model six tiny flattened balls of white modelling paste and stick these in place either side of the snout.

10 To make Cow's arms, split 15g (½oz) of the pale yellow sugarpaste in half. Model long teardrop shapes and stick these onto the side of Cow, smoothing them in at the top to remove the join. Model a tiny teardrop for the end of each and roll a thin sausage for a curl on the centre.

11 With 7g (¼oz) of the pale yellow paste make her tail. Split another 15g (½oz) in half and model two teardrop shapes for Cow's legs. Stick these in position, pressing the rounded end flat, and add a little curl made from thinly rolled sausage shapes as you did for the arms.

12 Colour 30g (1oz) of the modelling paste brown. Using the template (see p.93) thinly roll out and cut two patches for Cow's back. Smooth around the cut edge of each one to soften it, and then stick it in place with a little sugar glue. Model two small horns for the top of her head and four tiny teardrops for the end of her tail out of brown trimmings. Colour 7g (¼oz) of the sugarpaste dark pink and shape into flattened ovals to fill each nostril with.

13 To make Cow's ears, first colour 15g (½oz) of the modelling paste pale yellow. Split this in half and roll them into long teardrop shapes. Press each a little flat and indent them down the centre using your finger. Stick them against Cow's head, holding them for a few moments until they are secure. To support the ears as they dry, wedge a small piece of foam sponge underneath each one.

14 Colour a small ball of modelling paste dark grey using black and use this to make the hooves. Model small teardrop shapes first, then cut into each point. Colour a minute amount of modelling paste black and roll four pupils, sticking two of them onto Cow's eyes. Put aside the others for Chicken.

15 Roll the remaining pale pink sugarpaste into a ball and stick this onto the front of Cow. To make her udders, colour 7g (¼oz) of the modelling paste pale pink and split it into four pieces. Roll each into a sausage shape and pinch around one end to narrow it. Stick the udders in place and support them with foam pieces until they are dry.

MODELLING CHICKEN

16 To make Chicken, start by modelling his body using 22g (¾oz) of the white modelling paste. Make a teardrop shape, twisting a neck up at the point and then stick this in place against the side of Cow. Smooth the front down and out at the base.

17 With just under 7g (¼oz) of white modelling paste, model two eyes, put them aside and then make three teardrops for Chicken's tail. Split the remainder in half and use it to make the two arms. To do this, roll thin sausages and round off one end of each. Press the rounded ends flat and make small cuts to separate the thumb and fingers. Bend the arms halfway up to create elbows, round off the shoulders and then stick them against the top of his body.

18 Colour half of the remaining modelling paste bright yellow and model Chicken's beak. Leave it to set for a few moments, then stick it onto the side of Cow just above Chicken's neck. Support it underneath with a foam piece until it is dry. Next, assemble Chicken's eyes and stick them in place close together.

19 Colour a pea-sized amount of the remaining modelling paste orange using red and yellow food colouring paste, and then colour the rest of the paste red. Using just over half of the red paste, model three teardrop shapes and stick these together. Press them flat and smooth out the join before positioning them on Chicken's head. Use the remaining red to make two more teardrop shapes and stick them together as before, then stick them under Chicken's beak, against his neck.

20 With the pea-sized amount of orange paste, roll two long sausages that each taper to a point and stick them onto Chicken to create his legs. For his feet, model two more slightly smaller sausages that also taper, bend them in half and then stick them onto the ends of Chicken's legs.

Use this step-by-step guide to create Cow's udders.

Here are the components that are needed to make Chicken.

Turn Chicken's hands palm up when sticking in place.

Bugs Bunny

As the superstar of the cast, this carrot-chomping sophisticate is always one mischievous hop ahead of the other Looney Tunes characters.

CAKE AND DECORATION

20cm (8in) round cake (see p.11)

30cm (12in) round cake board

440g (14oz/1¾ cups) buttercream

1.375kg (2¾lb) sugarpaste (rolled fondant)

Green, black, orange and pink food colouring pastes

Icing (confectioner's) sugar in a sugar shaker

90g (3oz) modelling paste

Sugar glue

Sugar stick or length of raw, dried spaghetti

EQUIPMENT

Sharp knife

Large rolling pin

Ball or bone tool

A few cocktail sticks (toothpicks)

Brush for sugar glue

Small pieces of foam sponge

TIME SAVING TIP
Keep the round shape of the cake and cover it green. Model a small pile of carrots on the top for Bugs Bunny to pop out of.

CUTTING AND COVERING THE CAKE

1 Trim the crust from the cake and slice the top flat where the cake has risen. Cut off the top edge all the way round, cutting down and out to the base of the cake to make a conical shape. Keep the cut pieces quite large, turn them upside down and arrange them on the top of the cake to make the pile shape.

2 Sandwich the cake pieces onto the top of the cake with buttercream, then spread a thin layer of buttercream over the surface of the cake to help the sugarpaste (rolled fondant) stick. Position the cake on the cake board.

3 Colour 875g (1¾lb) of the sugarpaste bright green. Put aside 30g (1oz), then roll out the remainder and use it to cover the cake and cake board completely. Smooth around the shape, stretching out any pleats, and trim excess from around the edge of the cake board. Reserve the trimmings for later.

MAKING THE CARROTS

4 Colour the remaining sugarpaste orange. Model different-sized carrots by rolling them into long, teardrop shapes. Press into the full end of each with a ball or bone tool and mark lines by rolling a knife across the surface. Position each carrot as soon as it is made, covering around the base of the cake first and then building up around the sides to the top. Leave a small gap at the top of the cake for Bugs Bunny to slot into.

Once you have trimmed and cut the cake sides, pile cut pieces on top.

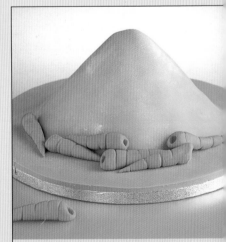

Position the carrots by working around the base first, building up around the sides and then covering the top.

MAKING BUGS BUNNY'S HEAD

5 Colour 70g (2¼oz) of the modelling paste grey using a touch of black food colouring paste. To shape Bugs Bunny's head, roll 30g (1oz) of the paste into a ball and pinch from the centre to the top to narrow it until the top of the head is quite high. Push in a cocktail stick (toothpick) on the underside to create a hole for the sugar stick or length of raw, dried spaghetti to go into later, remove the cocktail stick and put the head aside to dry.

MODELLING BUGS BUNNY'S BODY

6 Model Bugs Bunny's body and arms in one piece using 22g (¾oz) of the grey modelling paste. Start with a small sausage and roll both ends to lengthen and pull out the arms. Pinch up a neck at the centre, creating small dips either side to round the shoulders. Bend each arm halfway up and pinch gently to create elbows. Press at the front to flatten the chest area a little and slot into place on the top of the cake, securing with sugar glue.

7 Push a sugar stick down through the neck, leaving at least 2cm (¾in) protruding from the top to help hold Bugs Bunny's head in place later. With a small piece of white modelling paste, shape the patch for his neck and then stick it in place.

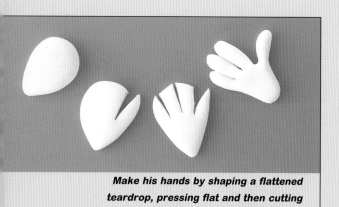

Model Bugs Bunny's arms and neck. Add the white patch at his neck area and make flattened white circles for cuffs when positioned on top of the cake.

8 Split just over 7g (¼oz) of the white modelling paste in half and use it to make the two hands. To make the hand holding the carrot, first model a small ball for the cuff and press into the centre with the small end of the ball or bone tool. Stick the flat side of this onto the end of his arm. For the actual hand, form a teardrop shape and press it slightly flat. Make a cut over to one side for the thumb, and then cut twice along the top to separate the fingers. Pinch gently to remove the ridges and then round off the tip of each finger. Press into the palm to round off the hand, bend it into position and stick it in place as soon as it is made, supporting it with a foam piece until it is completely dry. Break off the tip of one carrot and wrap the fingers around it. Make the other cuff and hand in exactly the same way and then position as shown in the finished picture, palm up with the thumb bent upwards.

Make his hands by shaping a flattened teardrop, pressing flat and then cutting and shaping fingers and a thumb.

9 To make the white mouth area, model a sausage using 7g (¼oz) of the white modelling paste and press it flat. Stick this onto the base of Bugs Bunny's head, smoothing it up and around the sides. Push down at the nose to create a dip and pinch down gently at the chin. To create fur, shape small, flattened teardrop shapes and stick them over the top of the mouth area, building up little by little.

10 At Bugs Bunny's nose area, stick two small, flattened balls of grey one on top of the other. Then split a small pea-sized amount of white in half, roll the pieces into ball shapes and use them for his muzzle. Shape his teeth and indent down the centre of them using the back of a knife. For his eyes, model two flattened ovals of white and stick these onto his face, spaced so that they are slightly wider apart at the top.

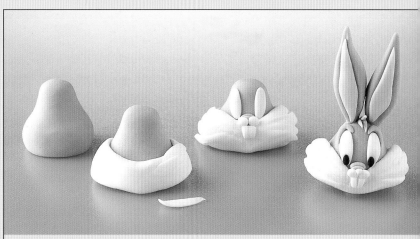

Build up Bugs Bunny's head gradually, working on the white mouth area first and ending with his ears.

11 Edge the top of each eye with a small tapering sausage of grey, and then make four tiny sausage shapes that taper to a point for his hair, sticking them onto the top of his head and smoothing them down at the back to remove the join. Colour a tiny amount of modelling paste black and use it to make two oval-shaped pupils. Colour another tiny piece of paste pink and make his triangular-shaped nose.

12 To make Bugs Bunny's ears, split the remaining grey modelling paste in half and roll each piece into a sausage that tapers at either end. Press in the centre of each sausage with your finger to indent it. Colour the remaining modelling paste very pale pink/peach using a touch of pink and orange food colouring paste and use it to fill each ear.

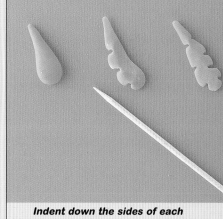

Indent down the sides of each carrot leaf with a cocktail stick.

13 For extra support, stick the ears together. Moisten the top of Bugs Bunny's head with sugar glue and then stick his ears on, holding for a few moments until they are secure. Turn out the tip of each ear very slightly, but make sure they are both well balanced. Press the head onto the sugar stick in his body and secure it at the base with sugar glue.

FINISHING TOUCHES

14 Use the remaining green sugarpaste to make all the carrot leaves. Model a small, flattened sausage first and then push in the tip of a cocktail stick down each side a number of times. Make a leaf for each carrot and position them to help hide any cake that is showing through.

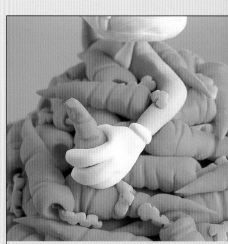

Slot the carrot leaves into the top of each carrot.

Tasmanian Devil

Taz is a wild, snarling whirlwind character who devours everything in his path. This is a perfect cake for a teenage son or even a much older man who is still young at heart!

CAKE AND DECORATION

25cm (10in) square cake (see p.11)

30cm (12in) square cake board

2.85kg (5lb 11oz) sugarpaste (rolled fondant)

Green, brown, chestnut brown, pink, black, blue and yellow food colouring pastes

440g (14oz/1¾ cups) buttercream

Icing (confectioner's) sugar in a sugar shaker

Sugar glue

EQUIPMENT

Large rolling pin

Sharp knife

Small brush for glue

A few cocktail sticks (toothpicks)

Small primrose cutter

TIME SAVING TIP

Make Taz with the tablecloth in front, but, instead of making the hotdogs, stack biscuits all around him, putting a broken biscuit in his hand.

CAKE BOARD AND CAKE

1 Colour 440g (14oz) of the sugarpaste (rolled fondant) green. Roll it out and cover the cake board completely, trimming excess from around the edge, and then put it aside to dry. (Reserve the green trimmings for later.) Trim the crust from the cake and slice the top flat where the cake has risen. Cut the cake into four equally sized squares and stack one on top of the other, making sure that the layers are well balanced.

MAKING TAZ

2 To shape Taz's head, trim all the way around the cake's top layer to round it off. To narrow around the sides and back of Taz, cut at an inwards angle around the base. Sandwich the layers together with buttercream, then spread a layer over the surface of the cake to help the sugarpaste stick.

3 Colour 1.25kg (2½lb) of the sugarpaste brown. Roll out 500g (1lb) of it and cut an oblong measuring 23 x 46cm (9 x 18in). Dust the surface with icing (confectioner's) sugar to prevent sticking and roll it up at either end. Position the sugarpaste against the front of the cake and unroll it around the cake, trimming any excess away from the join. Using sugar glue, stick the join closed around the top of his head and down his back. Then cover your hands in icing sugar and rub gently over the join to remove it. To create a fur effect, texture the surface using the flat of a knife.

Stack the pieces of cake on top of one another and then trim Taz's head and body shape.

Cover the whole cake with brown sugarpaste, then rub the join closed with sugarcoated fingers.

Once Taz's mouth area is stuck in place, mark lines on either side using a knife.

Add teardrop shapes around the sides of his mouth to create fur and indent lines with the paintbrush handle.

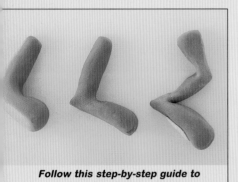

Follow this step-by-step guide to make each of Taz's legs.

4 Colour 90g (3oz) of the sugarpaste chestnut brown. Thinly roll out 30g (1oz) and cut a 10cm (4in) square for his mouth area. Stick this onto the front of Taz, just above the base. To separate the sides and back of his mouth, mark two lines on either side of it using the back of a knife.

5 Split 30g (1oz) of the white paste in half and model two flattened circles for Taz's eyes. Stick them on just above the mouth area so that they touch each other. Colour 280g (9oz) of the sugarpaste pale brown. Using 22g (¾oz), shape a semicircle and press it flat. Stick this onto the front of Taz at the base to create his tummy patch. Roll another 30g (1oz) into a sausage, tapering it at either end, and stick this just above his tummy patch, curving it up at both ends to make the bottom lip.

6 Split 125g (4oz) of the pale brown sugarpaste in half. Roll both pieces into long teardrop shapes and stick these either side of Taz's mouth, smoothing both ends into the surface. To make his muzzle, roll 60g (2oz) of the pale brown into a sausage and indent it in the centre to mark the crease. Stick this just below his eyes and indent whiskers into it using the tip of a cocktail stick (toothpick).

7 Shape the remaining pale brown into teardrop shapes and use these to build up fur on his mouth. To remove the joins, smooth them in with a little sugar glue, then rub gently with a little icing sugar. Mark lines on the pieces using the paintbrush handle.

8 To make his tongue, colour 15g (½oz) of the sugarpaste salmon pink using pink with a touch of chestnut brown. Model a ball and press it flat, then mark at the top and down the centre with the back of a knife. Shape pointed teeth using white paste, curving each tooth slightly before sticking in place.

9 Split 30g (1oz) of the brown sugarpaste in half and roll the pieces into two sausages that taper at either end. Use them to edge the top of each eye. Next, split 15g (½oz) of the brown in half and model two flattened, oval-shaped ears. Stick these in place and slightly indent the centre of each. Colour 7g (¼oz) of the sugarpaste pale pink and use it to fill each ear. To make his tail, roll 15g (½oz) of the brown into a long teardrop and press it flat. Make cuts along one end of it and stick it in place at the back.

10 Colour 30g (1oz) of the sugarpaste black. Split 7g (¼oz) in half and model two sausages to edge the outside of each eye. Also model two pupils and his nose. Split the remainder of the black in half and model eyebrows, making sure that they meet in the centre in order to create a 'cross' look.

11 To make his legs, split 250g (8oz) of the brown in half. Roll one half into a long sausage with a rounded end. To shape the foot, bend the rounded end and pinch out a heel. Press either side of the foot to lengthen it and round off the toe area. Make two cuts to separate the toes and pinch gently to remove the ridges. Bend the leg halfway up, pinching it gently to create a knee, and then position it. Make the second leg. Colour 7g (¼oz) of the sugarpaste slightly paler brown and model flattened circles for the footpads.

MAKING THE TABLECLOTH

12 For the tablecloth, thinly roll out 185g (6oz) of the white sugarpaste and cut a 25cm (10in) square. Arrange this on the front of the cake board, pleating it up towards Taz and pulling the two top corners around his sides. Roll out another 100g (3½oz) and cut a strip measuring 12 x 25cm (5 x 10in). Fold pleats into it and arrange it around the back of Taz, pulling the two ends around. Colour 100g (3½oz) of the sugarpaste blue. Thinly roll out a little at a time and cut squares to make up the tablecloth's chequered pattern.

MAKING THE HOTDOGS

13 Colour 250g (8oz) of the sugarpaste golden brown using brown with a touch of yellow. To make the hotdogs, split 100g (3½oz) of the paste into two pieces and roll them into sausage shapes, pressing them flat to make each bun base. Colour the remaining sugarpaste pale yellow. Roll out and cut two oblong shapes for the cheese.

14 Split the remaining chestnut brown in half and roll it to create the two sausages. Thinly roll out the green trimmings and cut out flower shapes using the primrose cutter. Chop these and drape them over the sausages. Put aside 7g (¼oz) of the golden brown, then split the rest and make the bun tops as the bases, but make them thicker. Stick the hotdogs in place.

ADDING THE FINISHING TOUCHES TO TAZ

15 To make an arm, roll 75g (2½oz) of the brown sugarpaste into a long teardrop shape and bend it halfway up, pinching out an elbow. Press the pointed end flatter to make the wrist. Stick the fuller end against the side of Taz to make his shoulder, and stick the wrist against his mouth for support. Make the second arm in the same way.

16 For hands, split 125g (4oz) of the brown sugarpaste in half. Model a long teardrop and press down on the top to flatten it a little. Make two deep cuts across the top to separate the fingers. Smooth them to remove the ridges and round off each tip. Stick the hand in place, smoothing into the surface of the wrist and make the second one. Cut up the remaining golden brown to make crumbs and stick these over his mouth and the back of his hand.

17 Using the rest of the brown sugarpaste, model different-sized teardrop shapes and use these for the fur, smoothing into the cake surface to remove joins. Position three pieces each on either side of his head sticking upwards. The fur on top of his head comes forward and is smoothed in at the back. Edge the top of each shoulder with smaller pieces of fur and stick tiny pieces of fur onto the top of each ear and at the elbows.

Arrange the tablecloth pieces, folding over and hiding joins with blue squares.

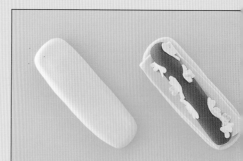

Assemble the cheese, sausage and lettuce shapes on the bottom bun.

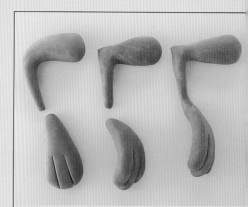

Model Taz's arms and position them. Then make the hands, smoothing the joins closed.

Wile E. Coyote

Yet again, Wile E. Coyote's clever tricks to catch Road Runner haven't gone to plan. No matter how cunning he tries to be, Road Runner always 'Beep-Beeps' another day.

CAKE AND DECORATION

20cm (8in) square cake (see p.11)

36 x 25cm (14 x 10in) oblong cake board

2kg (4lb) sugarpaste (rolled fondant)

Golden brown, dark brown, chestnut brown, lemon, black, turquoise, mauve and salmon pink food colouring pastes

345g (11oz/1½ cups) buttercream

Sugar glue

Icing (confectioner's) sugar in a sugar shaker

100g (3½oz) modelling paste

EQUIPMENT

Large and small rolling pins

Templates (see p.94)

Sharp knife

Small brush for sugar glue

Pieces of foam sponge

Cocktail stick (toothpick)

TIME SAVING TIP
Pile together white mini marshmallows and arrange them in a line to create Road Runner's speed trail.

CAKE BOARD AND CAKES

1 Colour 440g (14oz) of the sugarpaste (rolled fondant) deep golden brown. Roll out and cover the cake board with it, then press the large rolling pin over the surface to create ripples. Trim away excess, smooth around the edge to remove the ridge and put aside to dry.

2 Trim the crust from the cake and slice the top flat where the cake has risen. Cut the cake following the cutting diagram (see p.94). Trim a little from the depth of the smallest, then spread each cake with a layer of buttercream to help the sugarpaste stick to it later.

3 Colour 1kg (2lb) of the sugarpaste golden brown. Using 625g (1¼lb), roll out and cover the two largest squares, trimming the excess from around each base. Mark deep vertical lines around the sides by pressing in with the side of a knife, then mark horizontal lines using the blade. Position the cakes at opposite ends of the cake board, near the edge.

4 Cover the remaining cakes in the same way, adding white sugarpaste to the golden brown for each layer so the stacked cakes are darker at the base and lighter at the top. Make sure that they are well balanced, and then stick them together with a little sugar glue.

THE ROCKS

5 To make the large central rock, split 155g (5oz) of the golden brown sugarpaste in half and

Stack the cut cakes before covering to check that they are level and sit straight.

Cover the two largest pieces with sugarpaste, marking vertical and horizontal lines on the surfaces.

Follow these steps to make the large central rock that Wile E. will lie on.

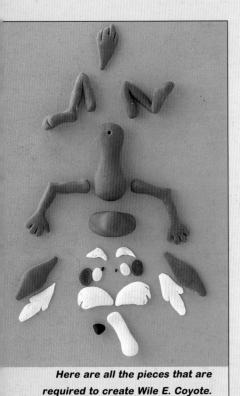

Here are all the pieces that are required to create Wile E. Coyote.

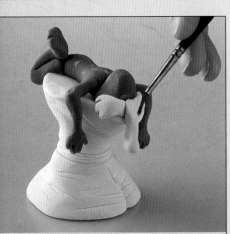

Fix Wile E.'s muzzle in place and smooth the join with the glue brush.

model two teardrop shapes. Press down on the rounded ends to flatten the shapes. Model a flattened ball with 15g (½oz) of sugarpaste and use it to sandwich the two pieces together. Mark the surface as before, then put it aside. Using some of the golden brown trimmings, make the tall rock shapes at the front of the cakes, marking horizontal lines on them, and then stick them in place. Use the rest of the trimmings to make the four smaller rocks on top of each stack and also shape small rocks to decorate the board.

THE BRIDGE

6 Colour 60g (2oz) of the modelling paste dark brown. Roll out half of this and cut a strip measuring 2 x 20cm (¾ x 8in). Mark even lines on it by pressing in gently with the back of a knife, taking care not to press in too deeply or the bridge may break when positioned. Using a little sugar glue, stick the bridge in place, leaving a gap in between it and the cake where the rope will be positioned later.

WILE E. COYOTE

7 Using 7g (¼oz) of the dark brown modelling paste, roll a sausage shape then indent it in the centre, rounding off each end to make Wile E.'s body. Stick this immediately onto the large rock, ensuring that there is enough room left for his head.

8 Split 15g (½oz) of the paste into five pieces, two slightly smaller than the rest. Put these smaller pieces aside for the arms, shape his head using one piece and then stick this in place using a little sugar glue. To make a leg, roll another piece into a sausage, rounding off one end. Bend the rounded end and pull it gently to lengthen it, keeping a rounded toe area. Pinch to shape the heel and pinch halfway up to mark the knee, pushing it in at the back to bend it. Place the foot down on the worksurface and make two cuts in the toe area, then stick the leg in position. Make the second leg.

9 Use the two smaller pieces to make the arms. Roll one into a sausage shape, rounding off one end. Press the rounded end gently to flatten it, and then make a cut slightly to one side for the thumb. Make two more cuts along the top to separate the fingers. Gently twist each finger to lengthen it and remove the ridges. Pinch halfway up the arm to mark an elbow and then stick in place using sugar glue. Make the second arm in the same way.

10 Colour 7g (¼oz) of the modelling paste beige using a touch of dark brown food colouring paste. To make Wile E.'s mouth area, using a pea-sized amount, model a teardrop shape and press it flat. Make cuts into the rounded end and bend it round, then stick it in position on one side of his face. Make another for the opposite side. Use more beige paste to model his long muzzle and stick in place, smoothing the join closed using the glue brush. Mark his mouth and a few lines on top of the muzzle using a knife.

11 Colour 7g (¼oz) of the modelling paste dark chestnut brown. Using two pea-sized amounts, model two oval shapes and press these flat to form his eye area. Colour a tiny amount of the modelling paste pale lemon and model his eyes, sticking them in place so that they touch each other.

12 Put a pea-sized amount of the dark brown modelling paste aside for later. Then using the remainder, along with two pea-sized amounts of beige modelling paste, make the ears using the template (see p.94). To stick each in place make a small indentation first using the end of the small brush, then stick the ears in position using foam pieces for support until dry.

13 With the remaining dark brown modelling paste, make his tail and stick it in place, indenting a small hole in the body first to help hold it in place. With the remaining beige paste, make two eyebrows. Colour a pea-sized amount of the modelling paste black and make two tiny pupils as well as his nose.

THE ROPE

14 Colour 7g (¼oz) of the modelling paste golden brown. Put aside a pea-sized amount for later. Then, using the remaining piece, roll out a little at a time into thin sausages. Using a cocktail stick (toothpick) indent diagonal lines on them to create a rope effect, then stick them around the bridge where you left space, and around Wile E.'s tail, cutting a broken end on each.

ROAD RUNNER

15 Using the remaining chestnut brown modelling paste, make Road Runner's legs and long, teardrop-shaped feet. Stick the legs against the front of the cake with one leg positioned slightly behind the other.

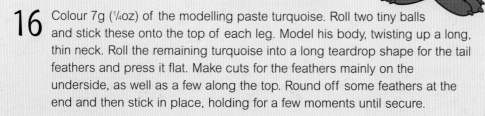

16 Colour 7g (¼oz) of the modelling paste turquoise. Roll two tiny balls and stick these onto the top of each leg. Model his body, twisting up a long, thin neck. Roll the remaining turquoise into a long teardrop shape for the tail feathers and press it flat. Make cuts for the feathers mainly on the underside, as well as a few along the top. Round off some feathers at the end and then stick in place, holding for a few moments until secure.

17 Colour 7g (¼oz) of the modelling paste mauve. Shape his head first, then his plume and make his two teardrop-shaped wings. Model two tiny flattened white ovals for his eyes and stick these in place with two sausages of mauve edging the top of each. Model two pupils using black paste.

18 With the remaining golden brown modelling paste make the beak in two pieces. Smooth the top part into the surface of the bottom using the glue brush. Colour a tiny bit of modelling paste salmon pink for his tongue.

FINISHING TOUCHES

19 Using the remaining white sugarpaste, model different-sized balls and stick these in position on the cake, piling them higher in various areas, to form Road Runner's speed trail. Lastly, stick the central rock, with Wile E. Coyote on it, on the cake board.

Follow the steps shown here to create Road Runner's tail feathers.

Position Road Runner's pupils so he is looking towards Wile E. Coyote.

After you have made the speed trail, position Wile E. on the board.

Daffy Duck

I wanted to make Daffy Duck in a watery scene, to capture some of the fun and adventure that always surrounds him. So here he is, riding the waves in a dinghy on a beautiful jade green sea.

CAKE AND DECORATION

25cm (10in) round cake (see p.11)

25cm (10in) round cake board

375g (12oz/1½ cups) buttercream

1.2kg (2lb 6½oz) sugarpaste (rolled fondant)

Blue, yellow, black and orange food colouring pastes

Icing (confectioner's) sugar in a sugar shaker

Sugar glue

90g (3oz) modelling paste

10ml (2tsp) royal icing

Light confectioner's glaze

EQUIPMENT

Sharp knife

Large rolling pin

Small paintbrush for glue

Foam sheet

Cocktail stick (toothpick)

Medium paintbrush

Template for the flag (see p.93)

Scissors

Paper piping bag

TIME SAVING TIP

Just make Daffy's head and arms, and then hide the empty dinghy with an awning made from a square of white sugarpaste.

COVERING THE CAKE

1 Trim the crust from the cake and slice the top flat. Centrally, from the top of the cake, cut a wedge at an angle, down to the edge and leaving a depth of 2.5cm (1in) at the lowest side. Turn this wedge over and position it at the highest side to create a deep slope.

2 At this highest side, trim away some of the underside of the cake, cutting at an inwards angle. Sandwich the layer using buttercream, then spread a layer of buttercream over the entire surface of the cake in order to help the sugarpaste stick.

3 Colour 500g (1lb) of the sugarpaste blue and 700g (1lb 6½oz) yellow. Knead the blue and 250g (8oz) of yellow together until it becomes green, leaving streaks of blue and yellow in it. Roll out and use it to cover the cake completely, smoothing around the shape and trimming away the excess from around the edge of the cake board. Pinch out waves along the front edge of the cake.

Cut a wedge from the cake and position it to create a slope.

Cover the cake with green sugarpaste and pinch out waves at the edges.

MAKING THE DINGHY

4 To make the dinghy, split 250g (8oz) of the yellow sugarpaste into six pieces and roll these into oval shapes. Using sugar glue, stick them end to end to create an oval. Roll out the remaining yellow sugarpaste and cover the oval completely, smoothing around the shape. Tuck the paste inside to create the seating area and also tuck the excess underneath the oval. Mark a line around the outside edge of the oval using a knife and mark little pleats along this edge using the tip. Carefully position the dinghy on the top of the cake, securing it in place with sugar glue.

5 Roll a long sausage for the flagpole using 7g (¼oz) of the white modelling paste. Bend it very slightly and place it on a foam sheet until it is dry.

MODELLING DAFFY DUCK

6 Colour 50g (1¾oz) of the modelling paste black. Using 30g (1oz) of it, model his teardrop-shaped body, pinching at the full end on one side to round off his bottom. Press the point flat and stick this into the dinghy so that it just comes up the inside and still leaves room for the flagpole.

7 Make Daffy's head next using 7g (¼oz) of the black modelling paste. Shape this into an oval then narrow it slightly from the eye area up to the top of his head. Stick this in place resting on the side of the dinghy, leaving room for the neck. Roll a pea-sized amount of the black paste into a sausage that is slightly thicker at one end and stick this in place to join the head to the body (the thicker end should be against Daffy's head).

8 Colour 22g (¾oz) of the modelling paste orange. To make Daffy's beak, model the mouth area first. Split 7g (¼oz) of the paste in half. Roll one half into a sausage shape and press this flat. Stick it onto the bottom of Daffy's face for his mouth area. With the second half, shape his beak using the step photograph as a modelling guide. Stick it onto his mouth and then smooth either side to remove the join. Stroke up the tip and press down either side of the beak. Mark nostrils using the tip of a cocktail stick (toothpick) and dimple the corners of the mouth using the end of a paintbrush.

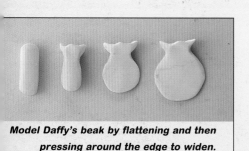
Use a rolling pin to lift the yellow sugarpaste and position it over the oval.

Make Daffy's body and then position it on the dinghy.

Model Daffy's beak by flattening and then pressing around the edge to widen.

Position Daffy's beak on his face and smooth either side of it.

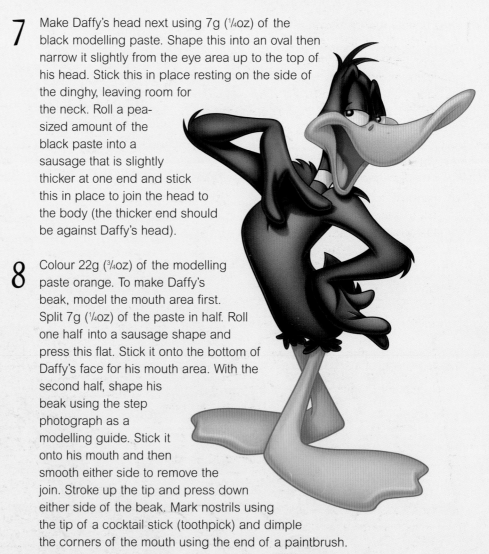

9 For his webbed feet, split the remaining orange modelling paste in half. Starting with a ball of paste, model a teardrop shape and twist up a leg from the point. Press the rounded end flat and shape it into the webbed foot. Stick this in place as soon as it is made using sugar glue to secure it, and then make the opposite leg.

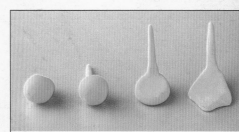

Use this step-by-step guide to how to model Daffy's legs and webbed feet.

10 With a little white modelling paste, model two flattened oval-shaped eyes and thinly roll out and cut a tiny strip for Daffy's neck. Also model his two small black pupils. Stick everything in place with a little sugar glue.

11 Split 7g (¼oz) of the black modelling paste in half. Using the step photograph as a guide, make an arm and hand with one half. Roll the piece into a sausage, rounding off one end, and press it gently to flatten it. Make a cut, slightly to one side for the thumb, and then make two cuts along the top to separate the fingers. Press gently on the fingertips to create fullness then stroke the thumb down. To mark the elbow, push in halfway up the arm and pinch it out at the back. Stick the arm in place as soon as it is made and then make the opposite arm in exactly the same way.

Follow this step-by-step guide to model each of Daffy's arms.

12 Put a pea-sized amount of black aside. Using the remainder, model Daffy's tail. First flatten a teardrop shape and then cut small uneven cuts at the pointed end for tail feathers. Stick in place on his bottom and smooth the base into the surface to remove the join. Model tiny sausages rolled into points for hair and stick these on his head, at his elbows, shoulders and the top of his legs.

FINISHING TOUCHES

13 Colour 7g (¼oz) of the modelling paste yellow. To finish the flagpole, roll out and cut the flag using the template (see p.93). Stick this at the top of the flagpole, wrapping it all the way round. Create pleats in it to suggest movement and then lay it flat until dry.

14 Stick a flattened ball of black onto the top of the flagpole, followed by a slightly larger flattened ball that is made using a little of the green trimmings.

15 Put the royal icing into a piping bag and cut a small hole in the tip. Pipe wavy lines along the waves. Using a damp paintbrush, immediately make brush marks away from the edge into the green, leaving a distinct line to resemble foam at the front of each wave.

16 When the cake is completely dry, paint a thin coat of confectioner's glaze over the surface of the sea to create a shine. Leave this to dry for around 10 minutes, then paint on another thin coat. Make a hole in the dinghy and down through the cake using the end of a paintbrush, and gently push in the end of the flagpole.

Paint the whole cake with confectioner's glaze to create a shine. Finally, push the flagpole into position.

MARVIN THE MARTIAN

The most peevish Martian in the universe, Marvin The Martian sits in his spaceship and declares war on Earth because we've blocked his view of Venus yet again!

CAKE AND DECORATION

Two 1l (2 pint) bowl-shaped cakes (see p.11)

25cm (10in) round cake board

1.2kg (2lb 6oz) sugarpaste (rolled fondant)

Blue, red, black, green, brown, yellow and pink food colouring pastes

280g (9oz) buttercream

Icing (confectioner's) sugar in a sugar shaker

Yellow and silver dusting powder (petal dust/blossom tint)

125g (4oz) modelling paste

Sugar glue

5cm (2in) sugar stick or length of raw, dried spaghetti

EQUIPMENT

Large and small rolling pins

Small knife

5cm (2in), 2cm (¾in), 1cm (½in) and miniature circle cutters

Medium paintbrush for dusting

Small foam sponge pieces

Cocktail sticks (toothpicks)

Small brush for sugar glue

Templates (see p.94)

CAKE BOARD

1 Colour 315g (10oz) of the sugarpaste (rolled fondant) deep blue. Roll this out and cover the cake board, trimming the excess from around the edge, and then put it aside to dry. Colour 15g (½oz) of the modelling paste black and put aside a minute amount to use later. Roll the remaining piece into a ball for Marvin's head. This ball will sink slightly when left because of the colour content, so put it aside for 10–15 minutes. After this, gently re-roll it in order to re-shape it, then put it aside to dry, preferably on a piece of foam.

THE PLANET

2 Slice the top off each cake where they have risen, then turn them over and trim off the crust. Using buttercream, sandwich the two cakes together to make a ball shape, then spread a thin layer of buttercream over the surface. Leave this to set for around 10 minutes.

3 Colour 875g (1¾lb) of the sugarpaste green. Using 30g (1oz), make small, flattened balls and press them over the cake surface. Re-work the buttercream or add extra to help the sugarpaste stick. Roll out the remaining green and cover the cake. Stretch out the pleats around the sides and smooth downward and around the shape, trimming the excess from the base. If you need to cut a pleat away, dust your hands with icing (confectioner's) sugar, press the cut edges together and smooth the surface over with your hands to close the join.

Trim the crust from each cake and put them together to make a ball.

Make flattened sugarpaste balls and press them onto the surface of the cake to make the craters.

76

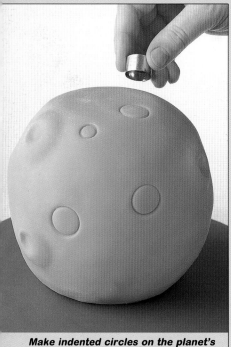

Carefully position the cake centrally on the cake board. Press into the surface of the planet using your finger to make craters, and then make indented circle patterns with the cutters. Protect the cake board with some kitchen paper and then randomly dust the surface of the planet with yellow dusting powder (petal dust/blossom tint) using the dusting brush.

THE SPACESHIP

4 Colour 45g (1½oz) of the modelling paste pale grey using black food colouring paste. Put aside 7g (¼oz), then model the remaining piece into a sausage shape, tapering each end. Press into the top to hollow it out slightly so that Marvin's body can be slotted into it later. Lift up the spaceship at each end using small pieces of foam to support it for a few moments until it has set. Gently roll the knife over the ship to mark lines, and then indent with a cocktail stick (toothpick).

Make indented circles on the planet's surface with circle cutters.

5 With the remaining grey modelling paste, roll out and cut two small oblong shapes for the door flaps, two small strips to edge the top and a 2cm (¾in) circle. Press the circle in the centre to indent it then, using a miniature circle cutter, cut a hole in the centre and circles around the edge. Roll a small ball and indent it in the centre by pushing the end of a paintbrush into it. Stick on the door flaps and strips with sugar glue and assemble the remaining pieces on the back of the spaceship.

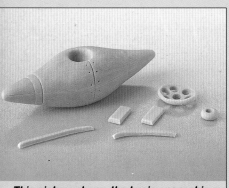

This picture shows the basic spaceship components made from grey paste.

6 Dust the spaceship with the edible silver powder then stick it carefully to the top of the planet. Colour 7g (¼oz) of the modelling paste red. Using half, model two elongated teardrop shapes and press each flat, curving the points around. Press the rounded ends completely flat, then stick them to the back of the spaceship using small pieces of foam sponge for support while drying. Make two more teardrops, a little smaller, and stick them on opposite sides.

MARVIN'S HEAD AND BODY

7 With the remaining red modelling paste, make the rest of the pieces for the spaceship, then shape a small oval for Marvin's body and roll a thin sausage for his sleeve, rolling one end to a point. Stick in position using small pieces of foam sponge for support. Push the sugar stick or length of raw, dried spaghetti down through Marvin's body and into the spaceship, leaving half protruding to help support his head when it is positioned later.

Build up the green helmet on Marvin's head by using the templates on p.94.

8 Colour 7g (¼oz) of the modelling paste green. Roll it out thinly and cut a circle using the 5cm (2in) circle cutter and stick it onto the top of Marvin's head, covering around the back. Roll out a strip of green modelling paste and cut out the helmet base using the template (see p.94) and stick it on the back of his head, smoothing the ends round to the front.

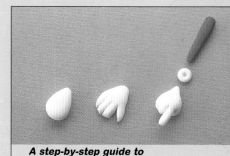

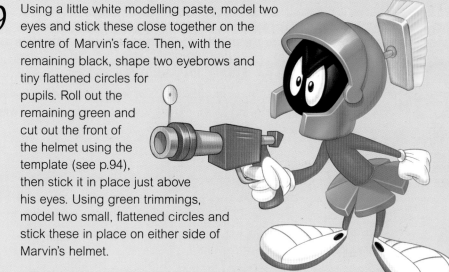

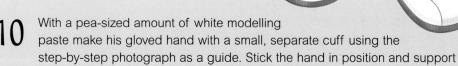

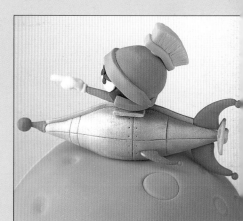

A step-by-step guide to modelling the hand and arm.

9 Using a little white modelling paste, model two eyes and stick these close together on the centre of Marvin's face. Then, with the remaining black, shape two eyebrows and tiny flattened circles for pupils. Roll out the remaining green and cut out the front of the helmet using the template (see p.94), then stick it in place just above his eyes. Using green trimmings, model two small, flattened circles and stick these in place on either side of Marvin's helmet.

The arm should be positioned at a slight angle. Support it until dry.

10 With a pea-sized amount of white modelling paste make his gloved hand with a small, separate cuff using the step-by-step photograph as a guide. Stick the hand in position and support it with a small piece of foam sponge while it is drying.

11 Split 7g (¼oz) of the modelling paste into two pieces, making one slightly larger than the other. Colour the smaller piece pale brown and the larger piece pale yellow. Model a small ball of the pale brown paste and stick it onto the top of Marvin's helmet to create the broom handle. Shape the remaining piece of pale brown into an oblong, 2.5cm (1in) long, and place this piece on top of the handle.

12 To make the brush, shape the pale yellow modelling paste into an oblong and then make cuts around the edge using a knife. Stick this onto the pale brown oblong and bend it slightly, then pinch around the top edge of the brush. Push the head onto the sugar stick, securing it at the base with sugar glue.

FINISHING TOUCHES

13 Colour the remaining modelling paste with various colours and use the pieces to model different-sized dome shapes for the planets on the cake board. Mix colours to create others – e.g. red and yellow for orange, pink and blue for mauve. For the swirled effect, knead two colours together until they are streaky. To finish the cake off, brush silver streaks over the board using the edible silver powder.

This shows a completed back view of Marvin and his spaceship.

Sylvester & Tweety

Sylvester tries so hard to catch sweet and innocent Tweety, never with much success. Yet again it looks like he won't have hold of Tweety for very much longer!

CAKE AND DECORATION

1l (2 pint) bowl-shaped cake, 1 x mini bowl-shaped cake and 15cm (6in) square cake (see p.11)

35cm (14in) round cake board

2.75kg (5½lb) sugarpaste (rolled fondant)

Mauve, black, red, yellow and blue food colouring pastes

440g (14oz/1¾ cups) buttercream

345g (11oz) modelling paste

Sugar glue

Icing (confectioner's) sugar in a sugar shaker

Edible gold dusting powder (petal dust/blossom tint)

EQUIPMENT

Large and small rolling pins

Small knife

3.5cm (1¼in) and 2.5cm (1in) circle cutters

Templates (see p.94)

Medium paintbrush for glue

A few cocktail sticks (toothpicks)

Fine paintbrush

Small piece of foam sponge

CAKE BOARD AND CAKES

1 Colour 440g (14oz) of the sugarpaste (rolled fondant) mauve. Roll out and cover the cake board completely, trimming excess from around the edge, then put it aside to dry. To make the halo ring for Tweety, roll out 7g (¼oz) of the white modelling paste and cut a circle using the large circle cutter. Cut another circle from the centre using the smaller circle cutter to make a ring and put this aside to dry.

2 To make Sylvester, trim the crust from the larger bowl-shaped cake and cut a flat area from where the cake has risen, keeping a rounded top edge. Turn this cake upside down and cut off a 2.5cm (1in) wedge. This piece will help form Sylvester's nose later.

3 Trim the crust from the square cake and slice the top flat where the cake has risen. Cut the cake exactly in half. One half forms the base of Sylvester's face. Cut the remaining half following the cutting diagram, (see p.94), to make Sylvester's neck and the top part of his head. Assemble this and trim off all edges around the cake. Place everything on the board and stick it together with buttercream. Then spread a layer of buttercream over the shape.

4 For Tweety, trim the crust from the small bowl-shaped cake and slice the top flat. This cake will form the top part of Tweety's head. Using 125g (4oz) of the white sugarpaste, model a piece to complete the bottom half of the head.

Trim and arrange the cut pieces of cake to form Sylvester's body.

Once all the parts of Sylvester's body a in place, cover them all with buttercre.

White sugarpaste completes the bottom of the head as well as the cheek area.

Cover Sylvester's body with black and form whiskers out of white sugarpaste.

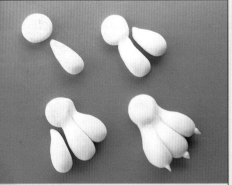

Follow the steps shown here to create Sylvester's hands.

Use a flattened circle and three teardrop-shaped pieces to form the basic foot.

Sandwich this to the cake using buttercream. Then model two small teardrop shapes and a flattenend ball, and use these to create the cheek and mouth area. Spread a layer of buttercream over the surface of the cake.

MODELLING SYLVESTER

5 Colour 1.17kg (2lb 5½oz) of the sugarpaste black. Using 500g (1lb), roll it out and cover Sylvester (apart from his nose), smoothing around the shape and trimming any excess from around the base. Using the template (see p.94), roll out 125g (4oz) of the white modelling paste and cut out two large whiskers. Smooth around the edge of each and then stick these to his head.

6 With 125g (4oz) of the white modelling paste, roll out and cut the remaining pieces for Sylvester's whiskers (see p.94). Split another 22g (¾oz) of the white in half and model two oval-shaped eyes. For his muzzle, shape an oval using 140g (4½oz) of the white. Roll this flat but thick and use it to cover the wedge of cake. Smooth it and indent a line using the side of a paintbrush.

7 Split 200g (6½oz) of the white sugarpaste in half. To make the hand that will grasp Tweety, shape one piece into a flattened teardrop shape. Make cuts to separate the thumb and fingers (see below, left). Using the end of a paintbrush, push in gently to make a small curve between each finger. Pinch around the base of each, removing ridges and making them narrow at the base and full at the tip. Bend the hand in position and put aside. Make the second hand. Pinch a ragged edge at the wrist to resemble fur and hollow this area out slightly so that the arm will slot in easily.

8 To make each of Sylvester's feet, first model a flattened circle using 22g (¾oz) of the white sugarpaste. For the toes, split 90g (3oz) of the white sugarpaste into three pieces, one slightly larger than the others. Model the larger piece into a long teardrop shape and stick this onto the flattened circle, smoothing into the surface to remove the join. Make two more teardrop shapes with the other pieces and position them either side of the larger one, smoothing them in. Make another foot and stick both in place. Using a little white modelling paste make the pointed claws for his feet.

9 To make Sylvester's back legs, split 280g (9oz) of the black sugarpaste in half. Model long teardrop shapes and bend them halfway up, pinching them to shape the knees. At the narrow end, pinch a ragged edge to resemble fur. Press the top of each leg a little flatter, and then stick them in place.

10 For his arms roll sausage shapes, using 125g (4oz) of the black sugarpaste for each, and bend them halfway up. Position them against Sylvester and stick in place, smoothing the shoulder area up against his body. Make sure the arm that will hold Tweety is further forward, and then stick his hands in position. Next, shape Sylvester's pointed hand claws.

11 For the tail, roll a long sausage of black sugarpaste using 90g (3oz), slightly tapering one end. Stick the full end onto Sylvester's back, twisting it round and securing it onto his leg. For the tip, model a teardrop using 22g (¾oz) of white sugarpaste. Pinch it narrower at the join and cut a ragged edge.

12 For his ears, split 22g (¾oz) of the black sugarpaste in half and model two teardrop shapes. Press them flatter and then press into the centre of each to hollow out slightly. Stick these in place, pinching up at the top of each to form a point. Using 22g (¾oz) of the white sugarpaste, make two more pieces to cover the inside of each ear in the same way and stick in position.

13 Using 22g (¾oz) of the black make his eyebrows, three long teardrop shapes for the fur on the top of his head and two fur pieces for either side of his face. Model two small oval-shaped pupils, press these flat and stick in place. Use black trimmings to make four tiny flattened circles to go on his muzzle. Colour 45g (1½oz) of the sugarpaste red and model his nose.

TWEETY

14 Re-work the buttercream on the Tweety cake or add a little more. Colour the remaining sugarpaste yellow, roll it out and cover the cake, stretching out pleats and smoothing downwards. If you have a pleat that will not smooth, cut it away and press the join together leaving a thin line. Rub gently with a little icing (confectioner's) sugar on your hands to remove the line.

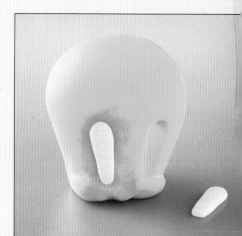

15 Using a finger, press in firmly at the eye areas to indent sockets, making them deeper and wider at the top. Split just under 7g (¼oz) of the white modelling paste in half and use it for the eyes. Model the paste into long oval shapes, press each flat and stick them into each eye socket. Colour a small ball of modelling paste pale blue and use it for the irises, then stick on two black oval-shaped pupils. Position Tweety on top of Sylvester's hand.

Make sockets by indenting the shapes with your fingers. Then fill these areas with white sugarpaste.

16 Colour 45g (1½oz) of the modelling paste peach using yellow food colouring paste with a touch of red. Using a pea-sized amount, shape Tweety's beak, indenting it in the centre using the tip of a cocktail stick (toothpick). Split the remainder in half and make two feet, cutting down the centre of each at the full end. Pinch gently to round them off and then stick them in position.

17 Model the paint tube using 7g (¼oz) of the white modelling paste. Stick a small ball at the top and indent it using the end of a paintbrush to make a hole. Using mauve trimmings, thinly roll out and cut an oblong to decorate the tube, edging it with a strip of black. Roll a mauve sausage and stick this into the top of the tube. To make the splats, model teardrop shapes and press each flat. Stick some together and rub to remove the joins.

18 Colour the modelling paste trimmings yellow. To make Tweety's arm, roll the paste into a sausage rounding off a little at one end. Model a hand as before but make it tiny. Bend the arm halfway up, pinching it out at the back to mark the elbow. Stick it in position, holding onto the paint tube.

19 When the cake is dry, dilute black food colouring paste with a little water and paint Tweety's eyebrows and eyelashes using the fine paintbrush. Apply the edible gold dusting powder (petal dust/blossom tint) to the halo with your fingers and stick it in place. Use foam sponge to support it until dry.

Arrange some of the paint so that it looks like Tweety has squirted Sylvester.

Tweety

Tweety is the most innocent and lovable yellow canary there has ever been. As he is the eternal target of Sylvester the cat, here he is on 'cat watch'.

CAKE AND DECORATION

25cm (10in) square cake (see p.11)

20cm (8in) square cake board

1.345kg (2lb 11oz) sugarpaste (rolled fondant)

Cream, blue, chestnut brown, yellow and black food colouring pastes

440g (14oz/1¾ cups) buttercream

Sugar glue

Icing (confectioner's) sugar in a sugar shaker

EQUIPMENT

Large rolling pin

Sharp knife

Ruler or straight edge

Small brush for glue

5cm (2in) and 2cm (¾in) circle cutters

Cake smoother

Piece of foam sponge

Ball or bone tool

2.5cm (1in) square cutter

Fine paintbrush

TIME SAVING TIP

The birdhouse still looks very pretty without roof tiles if you just mark a wood effect on the blue sugarpaste roof covering with a knife.

CAKE BOARD AND CAKE

1 Colour 720g (1lb 7oz) of the sugarpaste (rolled fondant) cream. Roll out 250g (8oz) and cover the cake board, trimming excess from around the edge. With the back of a knife, scratch lines over the surface to create a wood grain effect then put it aside to dry.

2 Trim the crust from the cake and slice the top flat where it has risen. Cut into four equal squares and stack the pieces straight, one on top of the other. To create the sloping roof, trim a wedge from either side of the two top layers of the cake. Sandwich the layers together with buttercream, then spread a thin layer over the surface to help the sugarpaste stick.

MAKING THE BIRDHOUSE

3 To cover the back of the cake, roll out 125g (4oz) of the cream sugarpaste. Indent even lines in it using a ruler and then turn the sugarpaste over. Lift the cake and place the back down onto the sugarpaste, making sure that the lines are vertical, and then cut around it. The piece should stick to the buttercream and so stay in place when the cake is put back onto its base.

4 Cover the sides and front of the birdhouse in the same way, using 250g (8oz) of the cream sugarpaste. To save marking the surface with your hands, hold the cake at the roof and at the base when you move it around. Then position the cake centrally on the cake board.

Once the cake pieces are stacked up, cut a sloping roof and sandwich them all together with buttercream.

To cover the back of the cake, turn it over and place it onto the sugarpaste.

5 Stick all the joins closed with sugar glue. Scratch wavy lines over the surface to suggest wood grain, integrating the join lines. Using both circle cutters, cut out two circular holes at the front and remove the sugarpaste.

6 Colour 315g (10oz) of the sugarpaste dusky blue using blue with a touch of chestnut brown food colouring paste. Thinly roll out 7g (¼oz) of this and cut a circle to fill the doorway, then roll out the rest and cut an oblong slightly larger than the roof. Lift it by rolling half back over the rolling pin and then cover the top of the cake. Use a cake smoother to neaten the edges.

7 To make the perch, roll a sausage using just over 7g (¼oz) of the cream sugarpaste and texture it as before. Press it flat at either end. Moisten around the edge of the small cut-out circle on the front of the birdhouse then slot the perch in, using a piece of foam sponge to support it until dry.

8 Using 30g (1oz) of the cream sugarpaste, cut strips for the fascia boards at the front and back of the birdhouse, mitring the join at the top. Thickly roll out and cut a strip for the bottom part of the finial at the front. Press in either side at the base to narrow it slightly and then texture as before.

9 Thickly roll out the remaining cream sugarpaste and cut strips to edge around the base of the cake. Mark a wood grain effect on them, integrating the join lines to hide them. Trim around the base, cutting in at an inwards angle and keeping a sharp edge along the top.

MAKING TWEETY

10 Colour 60g (2oz) of the sugarpaste yellow. Put aside a pea-sized amount then make Tweety's head (see left), blending the joins of his cheeks into the surface. Stroke the ball or bone tool over the eye area to create the sockets.

11 Colour a little sugarpaste black. With white and tiny amounts of blue and black, make Tweety's eyes. Model tiny oval shapes and press them until they are as flat as possible. Dust them with icing (confectioner's) sugar as you work.

12 Colour another minute piece of sugarpaste orange, using yellow food colouring with a little chestnut brown. For his beak, model two tiny teardrop shapes, one slightly larger than the other. Press down gently to flatten them slightly and then stick them at his mouth with the larger one on top. Using the pea-sized amount of yellow sugarpaste, model Tweety's hands.

FINISHING TOUCHES

13 Colour the remaining sugarpaste chestnut brown. Roll it out thinly and cut roof tiles with the square cutter. Stick a line of tiles along the bottom of the roof and then build up from the base. The second layer should start with a half tile and so on, so that the joins alternate between each layer.

14 With chestnut sugarpaste trimmings, edge around the base of the cake with thin strips and texture as before. With blue trimmings, model the ball and teardrop shapes to complete the finial. When the cake is dry, dilute a little black food colouring paste and paint Tweety's fine eyebrows and eyelashes.

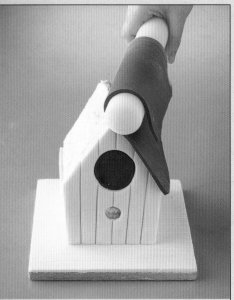

Cover the roof with blue sugarpaste using the rolling pin to help position it.

Use this step-by-step guide to model Tweety's head. Create the cheeks separately and smooth the join closed.

Cut around ten tiles at a time so that they don't dry out before being positioned.

With several of the best-loved
Looney Tunes characters on a wild,
reckless train journey, this fun cake
captures some of the typical cartoon
madcap humour it's known for.

CAKE AND DECORATION

25cm (10in) square cake
(see p.11)

35 x 25cm (14 x 10in)
oblong cake board

500g (1lb/2 cups)
buttercream

1.7kg (3lb 6½oz)
sugarpaste (rolled fondant)

Golden brown, black,
green, yellow, brown, pink,
orange, blue, chestnut
brown, mauve and red
food colouring pastes

Icing (confectioner's) sugar
in a sugar shaker

Sugar glue

390g (12½oz)
modelling paste

EQUIPMENT

Sharp knife

Templates (see p.94)

Large and small
rolling pins

Small brush for glue

2.5cm (1in) square cutter

No.4 plain piping tube (tip)

2cm (¾in) and 1cm (½in)
circle cutters

A few cocktail sticks
(toothpicks)

Pieces of foam sponge

Ruler

Small, pointed scissors

Fine paintbrush

CAKE BOARD AND CAKE

1 Trim the crust from the cake and slice the top flat. To make the engine and two carriages, cut a 12.5cm (5in) strip from the cake, and then cut as shown in the cutting diagram (see p.94). To make the hill, position the remaining strip on the centre of the cake board and trim off the top edge around the cake, using the trimmings to cover the cake board further.

2 Sandwich the top of the engine to the base using buttercream. Then spread a layer of buttercream over the surface of all the cakes, including the underside of the train and carriage cakes, to help the sugarpaste stick. Put the train and carriages aside.

3 Colour 625g (1¼lb) of the sugarpaste (rolled fondant) golden brown. To complete the hill, roll out and cover the cake on the cake board completely, smoothing around the shape and trimming excess from around the edge. With the golden brown trimmings, model different-sized angular rock shapes and then put them aside for later.

THE TRAIN

4 Colour 170g (5½oz) of the sugarpaste black. To cover the underside of the train, roll out 100g (3½oz) of the black and place the base of the train down onto it and cut around. Cover the top and bottom of each carriage in the same way and then put them aside, placed on a sprinkling of icing sugar to prevent sticking.

Cut the cake to make the engine and two carriages, using the trimmings to cover the rest of the cake board.

Use golden brown sugarpaste to cover the hill, trimming excess from the edge.

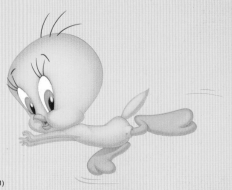

Use dark green sugarpaste to cover the train. Trim the base to reveal the black strip at the bottom.

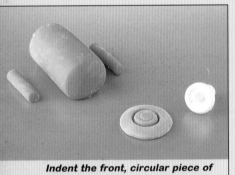

Indent the front, circular piece of the train using a circle cutter.

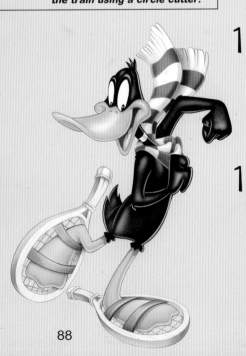

5 Thinly roll out 30g (1oz) of the black sugarpaste and cut a strip measuring 35 x 2.5cm (14 x 1in). Dust it with icing (confectioner's) sugar and then roll it up. Position it against the base of the train and then unroll the strip around the base. Trim any excess away from the join and smooth it closed using a little icing (confectioner's) sugar on your fingers.

6 Thinly roll out the remaining black sugarpaste and use it to cover both sides of the train at the door and window area only. Position the train cake towards the front of the cake board, securing it with a little sugar glue.

7 Colour 575g (1lb 2½oz) of the sugarpaste dark green using green food colouring paste with a touch of black. Roll out half and cover the train, smoothing down and around the shape. Trim around the base to reveal the black strip.

8 With the square cutter, cut out the window and door area on both sides of the train to reveal the black covering underneath. Cut out two circles for the windows at the front of the train using the end of the plain piping tube (tip) and remove the sugarpaste.

9 Colour 100g (3½oz) of the modelling paste black. To make wheels for the train, split 60g (2oz) of it into 16 pieces. Roll each piece into a ball, press it flat and then indent it in the centre using the circle cutters. Thinly roll out a pea-sized amount of the black paste and cut two circles to fill the windows on the front of the train.

10 For the dynamite, colour 100g (3½oz) of the modelling paste red. Put aside a pea-sized piece for later, then roll the remainder into thin sausages and cut them evenly. Indent into the end of each using a cocktail stick (toothpick) to make a hole for the fuse to slot in. With minute sausages of black modelling paste, make fuses for about a third of the dynamite, stick them in place and then put all the dynamite aside to dry.

11 To make the engine, roll 90g (3oz) of the dark green sugarpaste into a sausage measuring 6cm (2½in) in length and then stick this piece onto the train. Split 15g (½oz) of the dark green paste into three pieces. Roll one piece into a ball and press this flat. Indent it in the centre using the smaller circle cutter and stick this onto the front of the train. Roll the remaining two pieces into sausage shapes and indent into the front of each with the tip of the plain piping tube.

12 Roll out 45g (1½oz) of the dark green paste and cut a 6cm (2½in) square for the top of the engine. Using 60g (2oz), cut another square measuring 7.5cm (3in) and use this to create the roof, smoothing it at either side to make it curve downwards. With the remaining dark green, roll out and cut strips to add detail to the train. The strips around the engine are indented with the tip of the plain piping tube. Cut thicker strips for steps. For the grille, cut graduating strips. Stick these onto the front of the train, supported in the centre with a piece of foam sponge to hold it outwards. Finish with two strips edging the bottom.

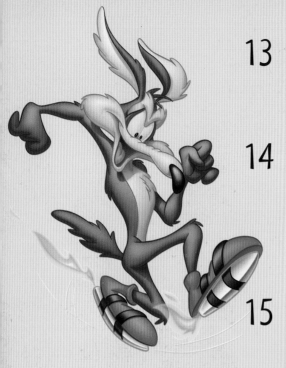

13 For the lantern at the front of the train, cut a small square of dark green using trimmings and stick this upright onto a base made from two small oblong shapes. Cut a strip to edge the top and smooth it round. Colour 7g (¼oz) of the modelling paste pale yellow. Using a tiny amount of this, stick a flattened ball onto the front of the lantern for the light.

14 Using 15g (½oz) of black and a small ball of green, make the funnel. Start with a ball of black at the bottom and press to flatten. Roll another ball of black and pinch to narrow at the bottom. Press the full end flatter and stick it onto the base at the narrow end. With the green, model a flattened circle and pinch up to form the top edge. Roll a sausage for the top, hollowing it out slightly. Model two bumpers for the front of the train and place a tiny piece of paste on each spot first, so that when you place the black bumpers on they will stick out slightly from the surface of the train.

15 Colour the remaining sugarpaste brown. Using 250g (8oz), roll out and cut pieces to cover the sides of each carriage, covering the two smaller ends of each first. To make the sides taller and to indent planks, press evenly with a ruler. Mark wood grain on the sugarpaste using a knife. Re-work the buttercream or apply a little more, and then press the sides into position, securing them with sugar glue at the joins. Indent small holes, edging each join using a cocktail stick. Arrange them on the cake board, securing them in place with sugar glue.

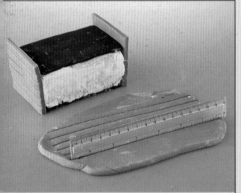

Cover the carriages with brown sugarpaste that has been indented with a ruler to create planks.

16 With the remaining brown sugarpaste, roll out and cut strips for the track, marking wood grain on them as before. Arrange the strips on the cake board, securing them with sugar glue. Cut up pieces to edge the train and carriages, slotting some underneath if there are gaps.

17 Colour 60g (2oz) of the modelling paste pale grey using a touch of black food colouring paste. Using 45g (1½oz), roll out and cut two long strips for the rails, again slotting some underneath where there are gaps. Mix 7g (¼oz) each of pale grey and white modelling paste together until streaky and shape the smoke. Stick this in place, supporting it with a small piece of foam sponge until it is dry.

18 Stick the wheels in place each with a tiny pale yellow ball on the centre. Using 7g (¼oz) of the black modelling paste, roll thin sausages with rounded ends and stick these onto the train wheels. Make two more that are much longer and use these to join the train and carriages to one another. Stick all the rocks made earlier over the cake board, edging the track.

MODELLING TAZ

19 Colour 45g (1½oz) of the modelling paste brown, 15g (½oz) pale brown and a pea-sized piece pale pink. To make Taz, first shape his body using 22g (¾oz) of the brown paste. Using the scissors, snip hair pointing upwards around his back and sides, starting at the base. Stick on two flattened circles of black modelling paste trimmings at his eye area. With white modelling paste, stick on two flattened oval-shaped eyes and finish these with two tiny black pupils.

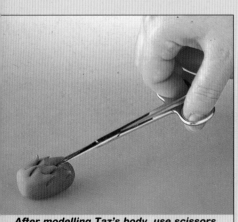

After modelling Taz's body, use scissors to snip up little points to create hair.

20 Split 7g (¼oz) of the pale brown into three pieces. Using one piece, model a sausage and bend it to shape a bottom lip. Shape the other two pieces into teardrops and stick these on either side of his face to complete his open mouth. Make cuts on either side to give a fur effect. Using a small ball of pale brown, model his muzzle, marking down the centre with a knife.

21 Model his tiny, black, oval-shaped nose. Then make an arm by rolling brown paste into a sausage shape and pinch gently at one end to round off the hand. Press the rounded end flatter and cut it to separate a thumb and fingers. Smooth out the ridges and push down gently at the tips to create fullness. Model two brown oval-shaped ears and slightly indent in the centre of each. Take the pale pink paste and fill each ear with it, sticking them into place level with his eyes. With a pea-sized amount of brown paste, model small, long teardrop shapes for hair and stick them onto the top of his head, smoothing in at the back to remove the joins and taking care not to break off the snipped hair. Fill his mouth and the rest of the carriage with half of the modelled dynamite, placing them all at different angles. Arrange lots of dynamite in the crook of his arm.

Fill Taz's mouth with dynamite and surround him with further sticks.

SYLVESTER

22 To make Sylvester, first split 7g (¼oz) of the black modelling paste in half. Using one half, shape his body, twisting up at the top to create a neck, and put it in the carriage. Model his head next and put to one side. Stick on a tiny white patch from the neck to the bottom of the body. Using a pea-sized amount of black for each, roll sausage-shaped arms, bending them halfway up to make elbows. Stick these on either side of the body and arrange them so that one arm is resting against the side of the carriage.

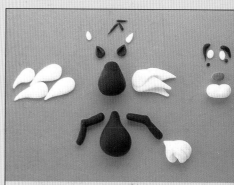

The basic components that make up Sylvester are shown here.

23 Split 7g (¼oz) of the white modelling paste in half. From one half, model teardrop shapes to build up Sylvester's fur on either side of his face, then model two oval-shaped eyes and two white patches to place in his ears. Using some of the black sugarpaste, roll tiny sausages with points at the end for his hair and then model eyebrows, two pupils and two teardrop-shaped ears, filling each ear with the white patch made earlier.

24 With the remaining half of the white sugarpaste model his muzzle, indenting a line in the middle of it with a knife. Make one hand by pressing a teardrop-shape flat and cut a thumb slightly into one side and fingers across the top. Smooth out any ridges and bend the hand round. Pinch gently at the wrist to create fur. Make his nose using red sugarpaste trimmings. Stick his head onto his body, holding it for a few moments until it is secure. Then place a dynamite stick in his hand and roll a long fuse to go inside the stick. Mix red and yellow modelling paste together until streaky to make the tiny flame. Stick this on the end of the fuse. Fill the carriage with the remaining dynamite, securing each in place with a little sugar glue.

Stick dynamite in Sylvester's hand and then fill all the carriages.

MODELLING BUGS BUNNY

25 See pp.60–3 for instructions on how to make Bugs Bunny, but make him much smaller here so that he fits into the train (you will need no more than 7g (¼oz) of paste to complete him). Once his basic shape has been

finished, stick his head in one of the side windows of the train, making sure that you tilt it out slightly. Then hold onto it for a few moments until it is completely secure.

26 To make Bugs Bunny's open mouth, stick a tiny flattened piece of black modelling paste onto the mouth area. Then the white part of the mouth should be made in two separate pieces. First roll a small sausage, making it thinner in the centre to form the chin area, and stick it onto his face. Model two tiny long white teardrop shapes for the top of his mouth and stick the points at his nose, smoothing the full end into the surface to remove the join. To finish off, add a tiny pink tongue to the inside of his mouth before modelling his teeth.

MAKING TWEETY

27 To make Tweety, colour a tiny ball of modelling paste bright yellow. Model two tiny hands first, making cuts with a knife, and stick these in place at the base of the front window nearest to Bugs Bunny. Shape Tweety's teardrop-shaped head and stick on two tiny teardrops for his cheeks, smoothing either side to remove the joins.

Stick Bugs Bunny's ears against the side of the train for support.

28 Make his eyes using tiny white oval shapes pressed flat, and then stick them in position just above the cheeks. Colour a pea-sized amount of modelling paste blue and, using a minute amount, make the tiny irises. Add black pupils, pressing each as flat as possible and use icing (confectioner's) sugar to prevent sticking. Colour 7g (¼oz) of the modelling paste orange and use a tiny piece to model the beak. Dilute a little black food colouring paste with water and paint Tweety's eyelashes and eyebrows using the fine paintbrush.

WILE E. COYOTE

29 Colour a pea-sized amount of the modelling paste chestnut brown to model Wile E. Coyote's eyes. Using this and the remaining brown and pale brown pastes, make Wile. To do this, see pp.68–71 for detailed instructions but make him much smaller here and assemble him in an outstretched pose on the front of the train. Stick his arms behind him so it looks as though he is holding on tightly to the engine.

MODELLING ROAD RUNNER

30 Colour just under 7g (¼oz) of the modelling paste mauve. See pp.68–71 for instructions on how to make Road Runner, but again make him smaller and only model his neck and head with teardrop shapes for his plume. Stick him in the other front window.

Daffy Duck's beak should also be positioned against the train for support.

DAFFY DUCK

31 The final character to be made is Daffy Duck. See pp.72–5 for instructions on how to make him from the remaining black paste. Stick his head at a side window, holding it in place for a few moments until it is secure, and also tilting it out slightly at the top. Make sure that the head is set before making the beak. The beak is quite heavy, so stick one side of it against the side of the engine and use a piece of foam sponge to support it underneath until it is completely dry.

Templates

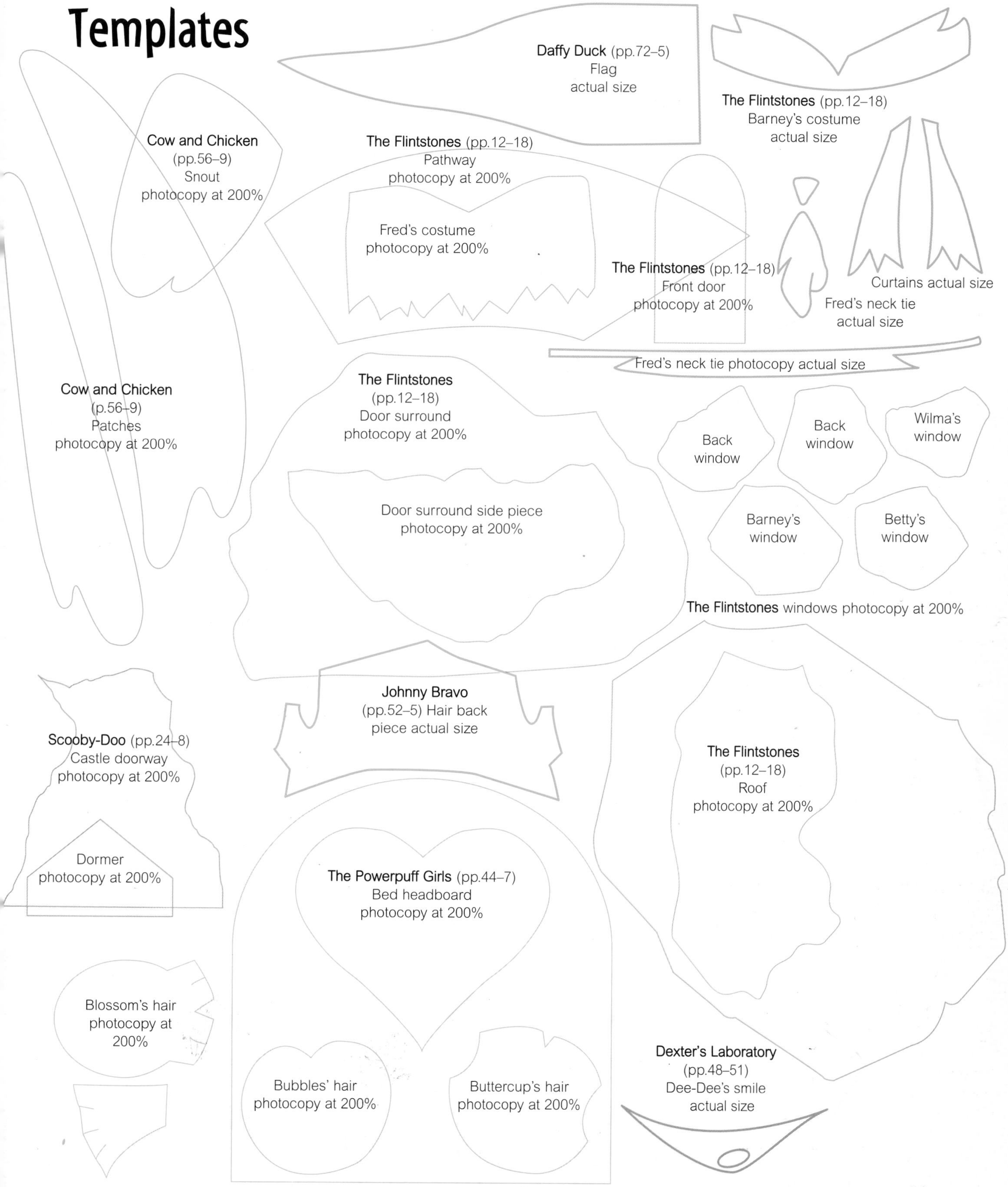

Daffy Duck (pp.72–5)
Flag
actual size

The Flintstones (pp.12–18)
Barney's costume
actual size

Cow and Chicken
(pp.56–9)
Snout
photocopy at 200%

The Flintstones (pp.12–18)
Pathway
photocopy at 200%

Fred's costume
photocopy at 200%

The Flintstones (pp.12–18)
Front door
photocopy at 200%

Curtains actual size

Fred's neck tie
actual size

Fred's neck tie photocopy actual size

Cow and Chicken
(p.56–9)
Patches
photocopy at 200%

The Flintstones
(pp.12–18)
Door surround
photocopy at 200%

Back
window

Back
window

Wilma's
window

Door surround side piece
photocopy at 200%

Barney's
window

Betty's
window

The Flintstones windows photocopy at 200%

Johnny Bravo
(pp.52–5) Hair back
piece actual size

The Flintstones
(pp.12–18)
Roof
photocopy at 200%

Scooby-Doo (pp.24–8)
Castle doorway
photocopy at 200%

Dormer
photocopy at 200%

The Powerpuff Girls (pp.44–7)
Bed headboard
photocopy at 200%

Blossom's hair
photocopy at
200%

Bubbles' hair
photocopy at 200%

Buttercup's hair
photocopy at 200%

Dexter's Laboratory
(pp.48–51)
Dee-Dee's smile
actual size

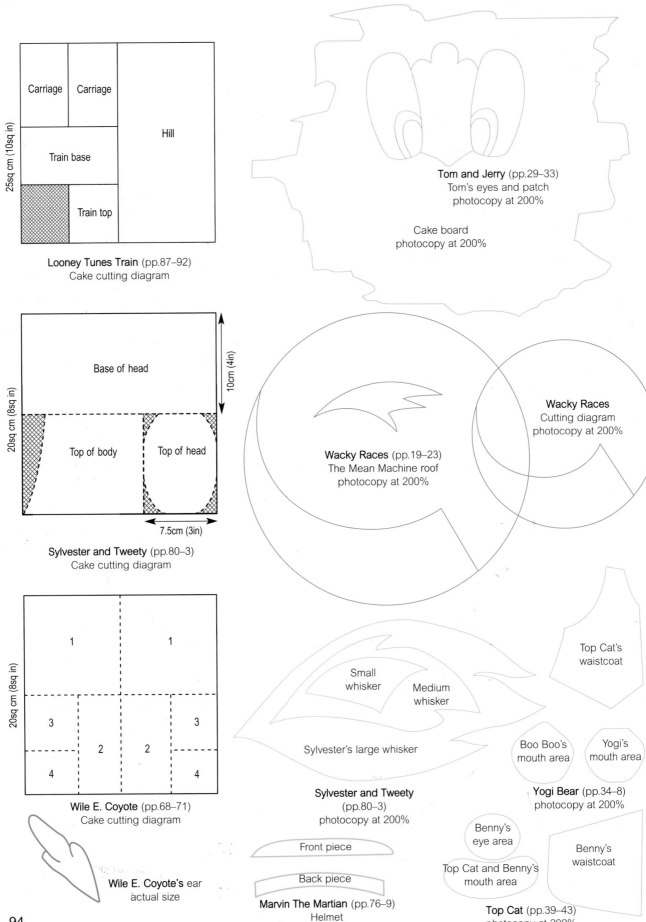

Looney Tunes Train (pp.87–92)
Cake cutting diagram

Carriage · Carriage · Hill · Train base · Train top

25sq cm (10sq in)

Tom and Jerry (pp.29–33)
Tom's eyes and patch
photocopy at 200%

Cake board
photocopy at 200%

Base of head
Top of body
Top of head

20sq cm (8sq in)

10cm (4in)

7.5cm (3in)

Sylvester and Tweety (pp.80–3)
Cake cutting diagram

Wacky Races (pp.19–23)
The Mean Machine roof
photocopy at 200%

Wacky Races
Cutting diagram
photocopy at 200%

20sq cm (8sq in)

1 · 1 · 3 · 3 · 2 · 2 · 4 · 4

Wile E. Coyote (pp.68–71)
Cake cutting diagram

Wile E. Coyote's ear
actual size

Small
whisker

Medium
whisker

Sylvester's large whisker

Sylvester and Tweety
(pp.80–3)
photocopy at 200%

Top Cat's
waistcoat

Boo Boo's
mouth area

Yogi's
mouth area

Yogi Bear (pp.34–8)
photocopy at 200%

Front piece

Back piece

Marvin The Martian (pp.76–9)
Helmet
photocopy at 200%

Benny's
eye area

Top Cat and Benny's
mouth area

Benny's
waistcoat

Top Cat (pp.39–43)
photocopy at 200%

Suppliers

The author and publisher would like to thank the following suppliers:

UK SUPPLIERS

Culpitt Cake Art
Culpitt Ltd
Jubilee Industrial Estate
Ashington
Northumberland NE63 8UQ
Tel: +44 (0)1670 814 545

Guy, Paul & Co Ltd
Unit B4 Foundry Way
Little End Road
Eaton Socon
Cambs PE19 3JH
Tel: +44 (0)1480 472 545

Renshaw Scott Ltd
Crown Street
Liverpool L8 7RF
Tel: +44 (0)151 706 8200
(Manufacturer of Regalice sugarpaste used in book)

Squires Kitchen
Squires House
3 Waverley Lane
Farnham, Surrey GU9 8BB
Tel: +44 (0)1252 711 749

OTHER DISTRIBUTORS AND RETAILERS:

Corteil & Barratt
40 High Street
Ewell Village
Epsom
Surrey
KT17 1RW
Tel: +44 (0)20 8393 0032

Pipedreams
2 Bell Lane
Eton Wick
Berkshire
Tel: +44 (0)1753 865 682

Sugar Daddy's
No.1 Fishers Yard
Market Square, St Neots
Cambridgeshire
PE19 2AF

Sugarflair Colours Ltd
Brunel Road
Manor Trading Estate
Benfleet
Essex
SS7 4PS
Tel: +44 (0)1286 752 891

Confectionery Supplies
31 Lower Cathedral Road
Riverside
Cardiff
South Glamorgan
Wales
Tel: +44 (0) 1222 372 161

Cakes & Co
25 Rock Hill
Blackrock Village
Co. Dublin
Ireland
Tel: +353 (0)1 283 6544

NON-UK

Beryl's Cake Decorating & Pastry Supplies
PO Box 1584
N. Springfield
United States
Tel: +1 800 488 2749

Creative Cutters
561 Edward Avenue,
Unit 1
Richmond Hill
Ontario, L4C 9W6
Canada
Tel: +1 905 883-5638

Ediciones Ballina Codai S.A.
Avda Cordoba 2415, 1st floor
C1120Aag
Buenos Aires
Argentina
Tel: +5411 4962 5381
Fax: +5411 4963 3751

The Cake Decorators School of Australia
Shop 7,
Port Phillip Arcade
232 Flinders Street
Melbourne
Victoria 3000
Australia
Tel: +61 (0) 3 9654 5335
Fax: +61 (0) 3 9654 5818

Cupid's Cake Decorations
2/90 Belford Street
Broadmeadow
New South Wales 2292
Australia
Tel: +61 (0) 2 4962 1884
Fax: +61 (0) 2 4961 6594

Suzy Q Cake Decorating Centre
Shop 4, 372 Keilor Road
Niddrie
Victoria, 3042
Australia
Tel: +61 (0) 3 9379 2275

First published in 2001 by Murdoch Books UK Ltd
Merehurst is an imprint of Murdoch Books UK Ltd
Design and photography copyright © Murdoch Books UK Ltd 2001
Text and cake design copyright © Debra Brown 2001
Licensed characters copyright © Warner Bros. 2001
Debra Brown has asserted her right under the Copyright, Designs and Patents Act, 1988.

ISBN 1-85391-924 1
A catalogue record for this book is available from the British Library.

Commissioning Editor: Barbara Croxford
Editor: Claire Musters
Designer: Cathy Layzell
Managing Editor: Anna Osborn
Design Manager: Helen Taylor
Photography: Clive Streeter
Photo Librarian: Bobbie Leah

CEO: Robert Oerton
Publisher: Catie Ziller
Production Manager: Lucy Byrne
International Sales Director: Kevin Lagden

Colour separation by Colourscan, Singapore
Printed in Italy by Giunti Industrie Grafiche

Murdoch Books UK Ltd
Ferry House, 51–57 Lacy Road
Putney, London SW15 1PR
United Kingdom
Tel: +44 (0)20 8355 1480
Fax: +44 (0)20 8355 1499
Murdoch Books UK Ltd is a subsidiary of Murdoch Magazines Pty Ltd.

UK Distribution
Macmillan Distribution Ltd
Houndsmills, Brunell Road
Basingstoke, Hampshire, RG1 6XS
United Kingdom
Tel: +44 (0)1256 302 707
Fax: +44 (0)1256 351 437
http://www.macmillan-mdl.co.uk

Murdoch Books®
Pier 8/9 23 Hickson Road
Millers Point NSW 2000
Australia
Tel: +61 (0)2 8220 2000
Fax: +61 (0)2 8220 2020
Murdoch Books® is a trademark of Murdoch Magazines Pty Ltd

Other books by Debbie Brown

Enchanted Cakes for Children
Favourite Character Cakes
Lovable Character Cakes

50 Easy Party Cakes
Creative Cakes for Men

Index

LC	1/02